Simulation of Groundwater Flow at Beach Point, Cape Cod, Massachusetts

Cape Cod National Seashore

Natural Resource Report NPS/NRPC/WRD/NRTR—2008/111

Larry Martin
National Park Service
Water Resources Division
1201 Oak Ridge Drive, Suite 250
Fort Collins, CO 80525

July 2008

U.S. Department of the Interior
National Park Service
Natural Resources Program Center
Fort Collins, Colorado

The Natural Resource Publication series addresses natural resource topics that are of interest and applicability to a broad readership in the National Park Service and to others in the management of natural resources, including the scientific community, the public, and the NPS conservation and environmental constituencies. Manuscripts are peer-reviewed to ensure that the information is scientifically credible, technically accurate, appropriately written for the intended audience, and is designed and published in a professional manner.

The Natural Resources Technical Reports series is used to disseminate the peer-reviewed results of scientific studies in the physical, biological, and social sciences for both the advancement of science and the achievement of the National Park Service's mission. The reports provide contributors with a forum for displaying comprehensive data that are often deleted from journals because of page limitations. Current examples of such reports include the results of research that addresses natural resource management issues; natural resource inventory and monitoring activities; resource assessment reports; scientific literature reviews; and peer reviewed proceedings of technical workshops, conferences, or symposia.

Views, statements, findings, conclusions, recommendations, and data in this report are solely those of the author(s) and do not necessarily reflect views and policies of the U.S. Department of the Interior, NPS. Mention of trade names or commercial products does not constitute endorsement or recommendation for use by the National Park Service.

Printed copies of reports in these series may be produced in a limited quantity and they are only available as long as the supply lasts. This report is available from the Water Resources Division Technical Reports Web site (http://www.nature.nps.gov/water/technicalReports/ReportsIndex.cfm), the Natural Resource Publications Management Web site (http://www.nature.nps.gov/publications/NRPM), or by sending a request to the address on the back cover.

Please cite this publication as:

Martin, Larry. 2008. Simulation of Groundwater Flow at Beach Point, Cape Cod, Massachusetts, Cape Cod National Seashore. Natural Resource Technical Report NPS/NRPC/WRD/NRTR—2008/111. National Park Service, Fort Collins, Colorado.

NPS D-393, July 2008

Contents

Figures

iv

Figures (continued)

Tables

Appendixes

Executive Summary

Computer modeling of the groundwater flow system underlying the Beach Point barrier beach was conducted to evaluate the potential for groundwater to flow toward, and discharge to, the East Harbor Lagoon under both existing conditions and with increased tidal flow to the lagoon. The elevation of the water table in the barrier beach fluctuates in response to tides in Cape Cod Bay. At high tide, water from the bay infiltrates into the barrier beach, causing the water table to rise. At low tide, groundwater drains from the barrier beach to the bay, lowering the water table. The amplitude of tidal fluctuation of the water table decreases with increasing distance from the bay.

Simulations of groundwater flow showed that the net flow of groundwater is toward Cape Cod Bay under current conditions of restricted tidal flow to the East Harbor Lagoon. The nearly constant elevation of the water surface in the lagoon provides a constant-head boundary for the water table in the barrier beach in the area adjacent to the lagoon. At high tide, the water table in that part of the barrier beach adjacent to Cape Cod Bay is temporarily higher than the water table near the lagoon, but the duration of the high tide is not long enough to cause a complete reversal of groundwater flow throughout the barrier beach.

Simulations of groundwater flow were also conducted to evaluate the potential effects of restoring tidal flow to the East Harbor Lagoon. The net flow of groundwater is from the lagoon toward the bay for all conditions that were evaluated.

Computer modeling showed that septic effluent, and any other contaminants that might be introduced to the groundwater system, from the developed strip along Rte 6A will always flow toward Cape Cod Bay. There is no indication that contaminants or nutrients from the developed area could be transported to the East Harbor Lagoon via the groundwater flow system.

Acknowledgements

Tom Cambareri and Scott Michaud (Cape Cod Commission) assisted with planning and design of the investigation. Their review and comments of earlier drafts and expertise of local hydrogeologic conditions were most helpful. Tom Cambareri assisted with the installation of the monitoring wells.

John Portnoy and Kelly Chapman (Cape Cod National Seashore) conducted most of the fieldwork, including installation of monitoring wells, surveying, monitoring water levels, and data collection and analyses. John Portnoy provided review and comment of several drafts of this report.

Charleen Greenhalgh, Gary Palmer, and Fred Schlipp contacted private property owners for permission to conduct this study on their land. Eleanor Collins kindly permitted us to install monitoring wells on her property.

Introduction

Tidal flow to the East Harbor Lagoon was abruptly cut off in 1868 with the construction of a dike across the inlet between the lagoon and Cape Cod Bay. Currently, tidal flow to the lagoon is limited to one 4-ft-diameter circular culvert, 700 ft long, underlying the Beach Point barrier beach and two highways (Rte. 6 & 6A) that connect the tip of Cape Cod and Provincetown with the remainder of the Cape.

There is concern that increased development of Beach Point could affect water quality in the East Harbor Lagoon. As small, seasonal cottages are converted to larger, more permanent residences, water use and septic effluent increase. Septic effluent disposal for residences on the barrier beach is by infiltration through on-site disposal systems (leachfields).

Computer modeling of the groundwater flow system underlying the Beach Point barrier beach was conducted to evaluate the potential for groundwater to flow toward, and discharge to, the East Harbor Lagoon under both existing conditions and with restoration of tidal flow to the lagoon. The study area is shown in Figure 1.

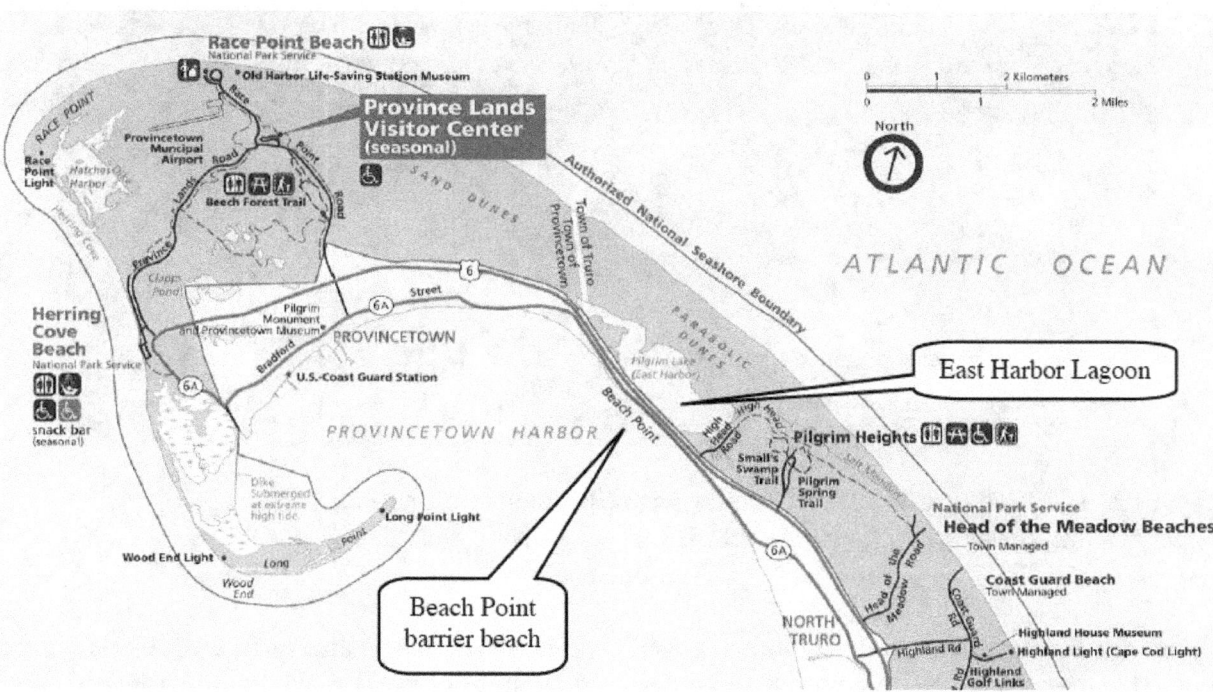

Figure 1. Location of the East Harbor Lagoon and the Beach Point barrier beach, Cape Cod, Massachusetts.

Groundwater Flow - Existing Conditions

A two-dimensional, cross-section model of the groundwater flow system underlying the Beach Point barrier beach was constructed to analyze the potential for nutrient-rich effluent from individual on-site sewage disposal systems on the barrier beach to flow toward, and discharge to, the East Harbor Lagoon (aka Pilgrim Lake). Staff at Cape Cod National Seashore installed three water level monitoring wells at each of two transects across the barrier beach. The computer model simulates groundwater flow in the barrier beach in the vicinity of Transect 2 (Figure 2).

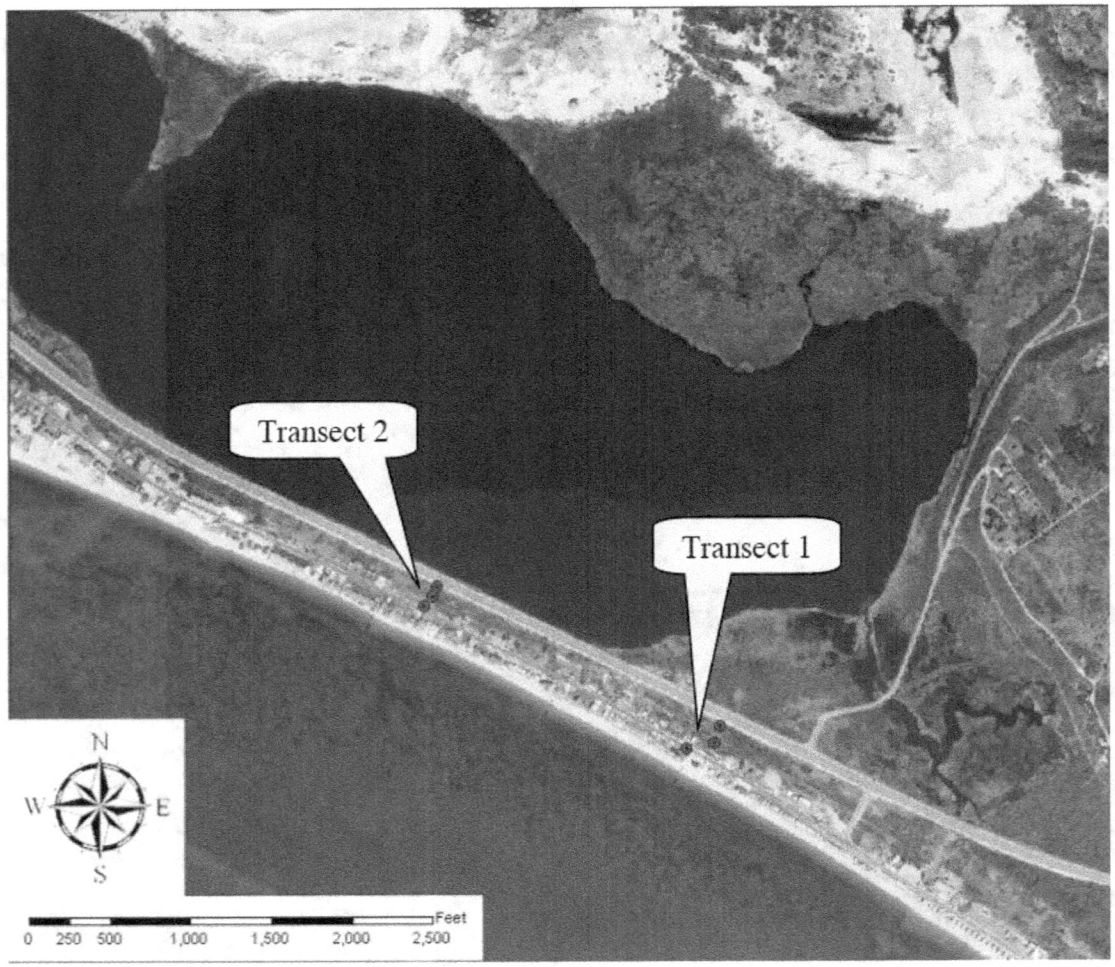

Figure 2. Location of water level monitoring wells along two transects across the Beach Point barrier beach.

Groundwater elevations in the monitoring wells on the barrier beach and surface water elevations in East Harbor have been monitored and recorded by staff at Cape Cod National Seashore since August 2007. The tidal fluctuation of water in Cape Cod Bay was obtained from records of the NOAA tidal gage in Boston Harbor (station ID 8443970). The tidal range in Cape Cod Bay is approximately 11½ feet. The tidal range in the East Harbor Lagoon is about ¼ foot (Figure 3).

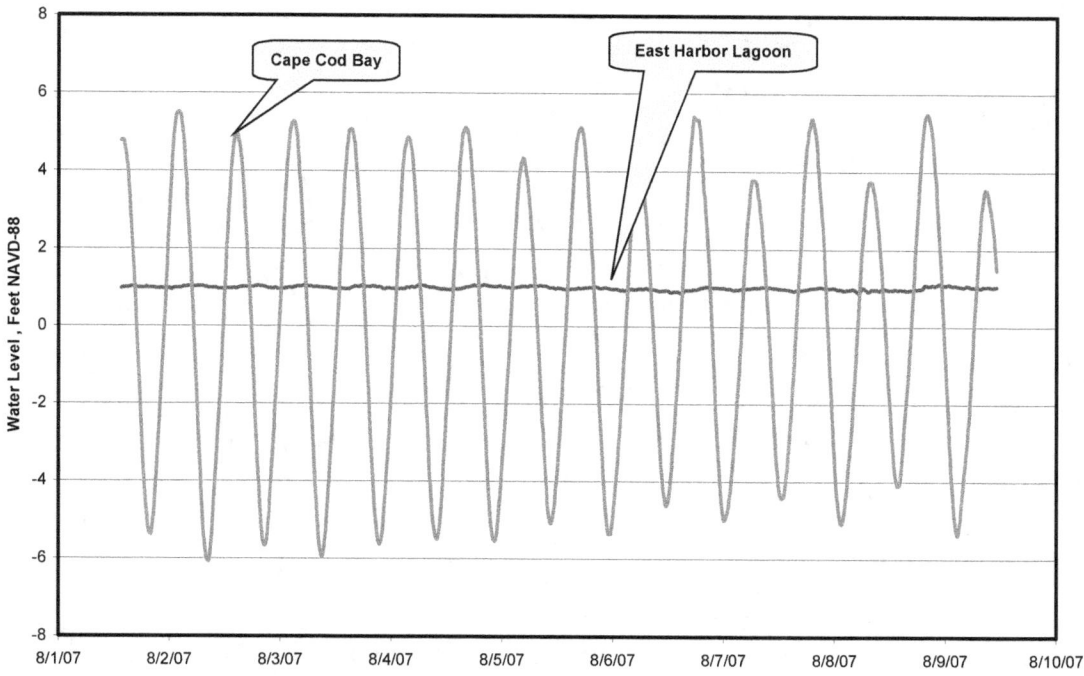

Figure 3. Measured water surface elevation in the East Harbor Lagoon and tidal fluctuation in Cape Cod Bay.

The elevation of the water table in the barrier beach is affected by tidal fluctuation in Cape Cod Bay. At high tide, water from the bay flows into the barrier beach, raising the water table. At low tide, groundwater drains from the barrier beach into the bay, lowering the water table. The amplitude of tidal fluctuation of the water table underlying the Beach Point barrier beach decreases with increasing distance from Cape Cod Bay. Figure 4 is a schematic cross-section through the barrier beach showing an approximation of the water table at high tide and low tide. The question of concern is whether the water table at high tide rises far enough and persists long enough to cause groundwater (and nutrients in the groundwater) to flow toward, and discharge into, the East Harbor Lagoon.

3

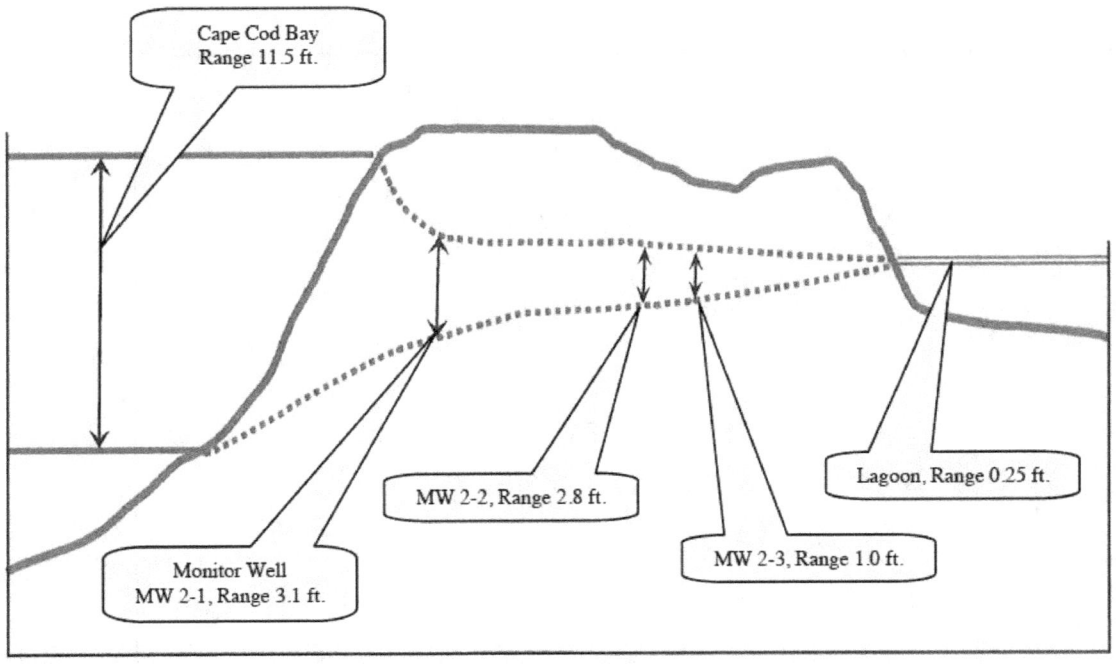

Figure 4. Schematic cross-section through the Beach Point barrier beach showing the observed tidal range in monitoring wells at various distances from Cape Cod Bay.

Model Description

The groundwater flow system was modeled using Visual MODFLOW, version 4.1. The computer model of the groundwater flow system has 2 rows, 22 columns, and 3 layers. Although the aquifer was modeled as being homogeneous and isotropic, it was necessary to divide the modeled area into multiple rows and layers for the model to run properly. The model has two rows, which are 1 foot and 100 feet wide. The row that is 1 foot wide is a dummy row that was included to make the model function properly. The software program for the model requires more than 1 row, column, or layer to function as a three-dimensional model, thus the need for a second row. The model has 22 columns, dividing the barrier beach into 20-foot segments from the bay to the lagoon. The first column is a constant head boundary with varying water elevation corresponding to tide levels in Cape Cod Bay. The last column is a constant head boundary with varying water elevation corresponding to measured water levels in the East Harbor Lagoon. The model has three layers with the bottom of the layers set at -10, -30, and -50 feet relative to sea level. The model grid and orientation are shown in Figure 5.

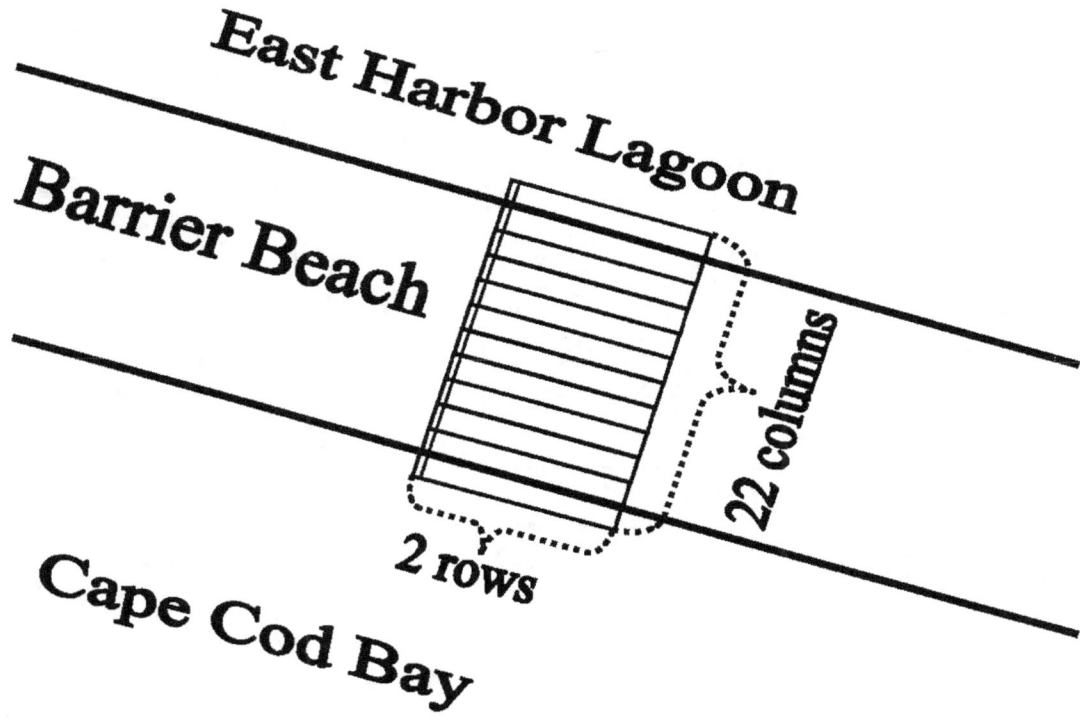

Figure 5. Orientation of the model grid across the barrier beach.

Source Data for the Computer Model

Water surface elevations for Cape Cod Bay were obtained from tidal records in Boston Harbor. Water surface elevations for the East Harbor Lagoon were recorded with a pressure transducer and automatic data logger. Water table elevations in the Beach Point barrier beach were measured and recorded at three monitoring wells along a transect from Cape Cod Bay to the East Harbor Lagoon (Figure 2), also using pressure transducers and data loggers. The monitoring wells along Transect 2 are at distances of 189 feet (MW 2-1), 243 feet (MW 2-2), and 279 feet (MW 2-3) from Cape Cod Bay.

Model Calibration

The modeled area was treated as being homogeneous and isotropic. All cells were assigned the same hydrologic properties. The model was calibrated by adjusting values for hydraulic conductivity and specific yield to reproduce observed water table fluctuations during the August 1-9, 2007 period. Goodness-of-fit was assessed by visually comparing observed and simulated water level data (Figure 6).

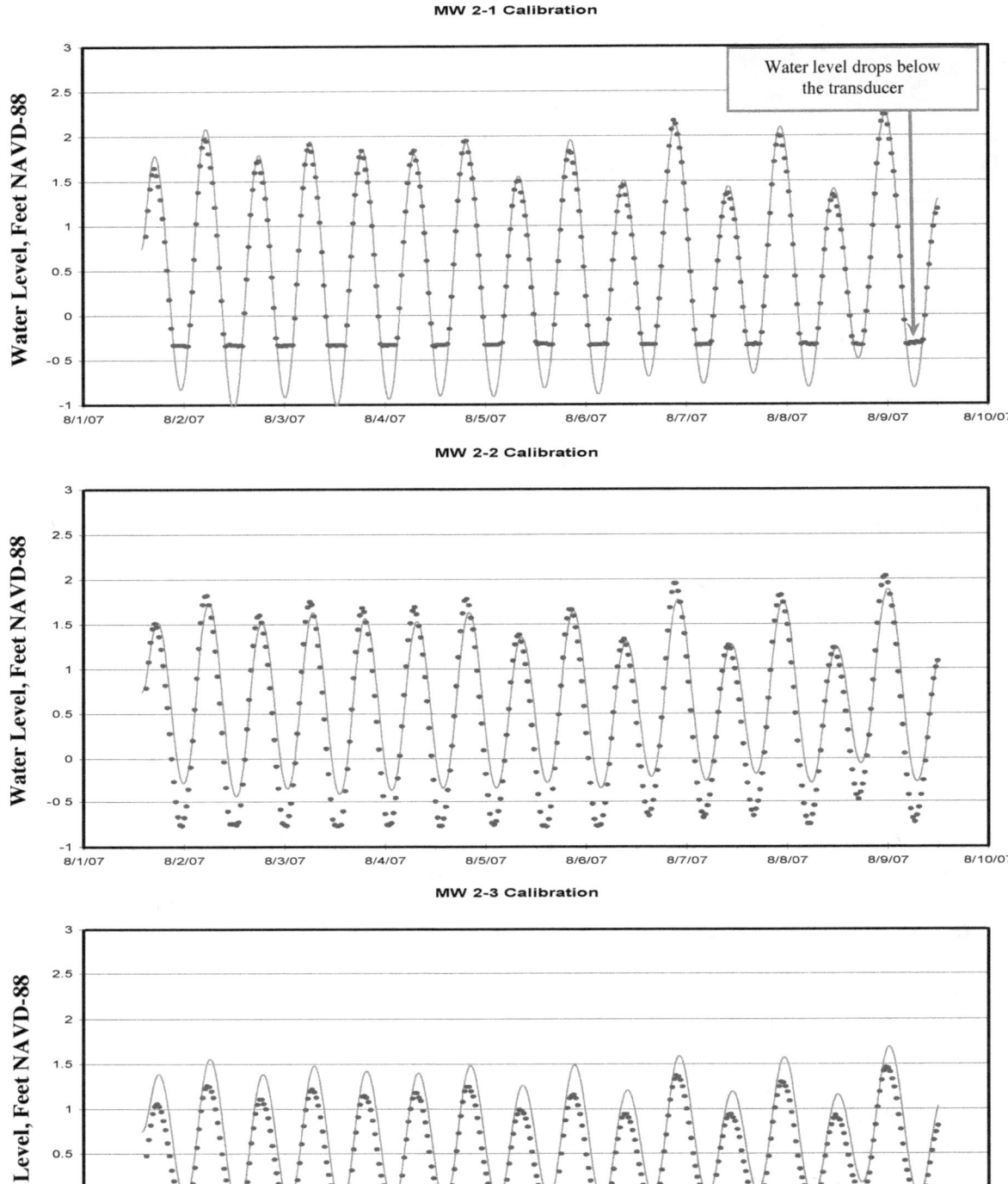

Figure 6. Comparison of observed and simulated water levels in monitoring wells. Solid red lines are the simulated water level. Blue dots are observed water levels in the monitor wells.

The best overall fit of calculated and observed data was obtained by assigning the hydraulic conductivity equal to 425 ft/day and a specific yield of 0.15. These are reasonable values, within the generally accepted range of published data for medium-grained sand

The water level in monitor well MW 2-1 drops below the bottom of the well at low tide. The datalogger continues to record values equal to the bottom elevation of the well until the well is refilled with the next rising tide. The result is a period of constant values at an elevation of -0.33 feet at low tide.

Calibration of a groundwater flow model was evaluated quantitatively by calculating the coefficient of determination (R^2) for a linear regression of the observed and calculated water levels. Because the water level drops below the bottom of the monitoring well in MW 2-1 at low tide, we can not use the entire period of record to compare observed and calculated water levels. Figure 7 shows the correlation of observed and calculated water levels for the last high tide of the calibration period, from August 8 18:30 to August 9 04:00. The R^2 values for the regression line of observed vs. calculated values for MW 2-1 is 0.99, for MW 2-2 it is 0.91, and for MW 2-3 it is 0.94.

The coefficient of determination (R^2) may not provide a good measure of calibration if the residuals between the calculated and observed water levels are evenly distributed above and below the regression line, as is the case for monitoring well MW 2-2 (Figure 7). The mean absolute error (MAE) provides another method of assessing the calibration of the model. The MAE is the mean of the absolute value of the differences between the measured and calculated water levels. The MAE for this model is 0.03' at well MW 2-1, 0.21' at well MW 2-2, and 0.20' at well MW 2-3.

Model Results

Groundwater flow in the barrier beach was simulated by running the model for a two week period. Limitations of the software version did not allow longer simulation periods. Simulated groundwater flow and water table elevations quickly (within less than a day) adjusted to the tidal regime of the bay and lagoon and thereafter followed a regular cyclic pattern corresponding to the tidal pattern.

At low tide, groundwater flows from the lagoon side of the barrier beach to the bay side of the barrier beach, with discharge occurring to Cape Cod Bay (Figure 8). The water table is nearly flat under most of the barrier beach. The water table on the lagoon side of the barrier beach remains nearly constant due to the nearly constant elevation of surface water in the East Harbor Lagoon.

At high tide, water from Cape Cod Bay flows into the barrier beach, raising the water in the near shore area and for some distance back into the barrier beach (Figure 9). The duration of the high tide is not long enough to completely reverse groundwater flow across the entire barrier beach. Instead, there is groundwater inflow from the bay and also inflow from the lagoon, with an area of temporary stagnation somewhere in the middle of the barrier beach, about two-thirds of the distance from the bay to the lagoon (Figure 9).

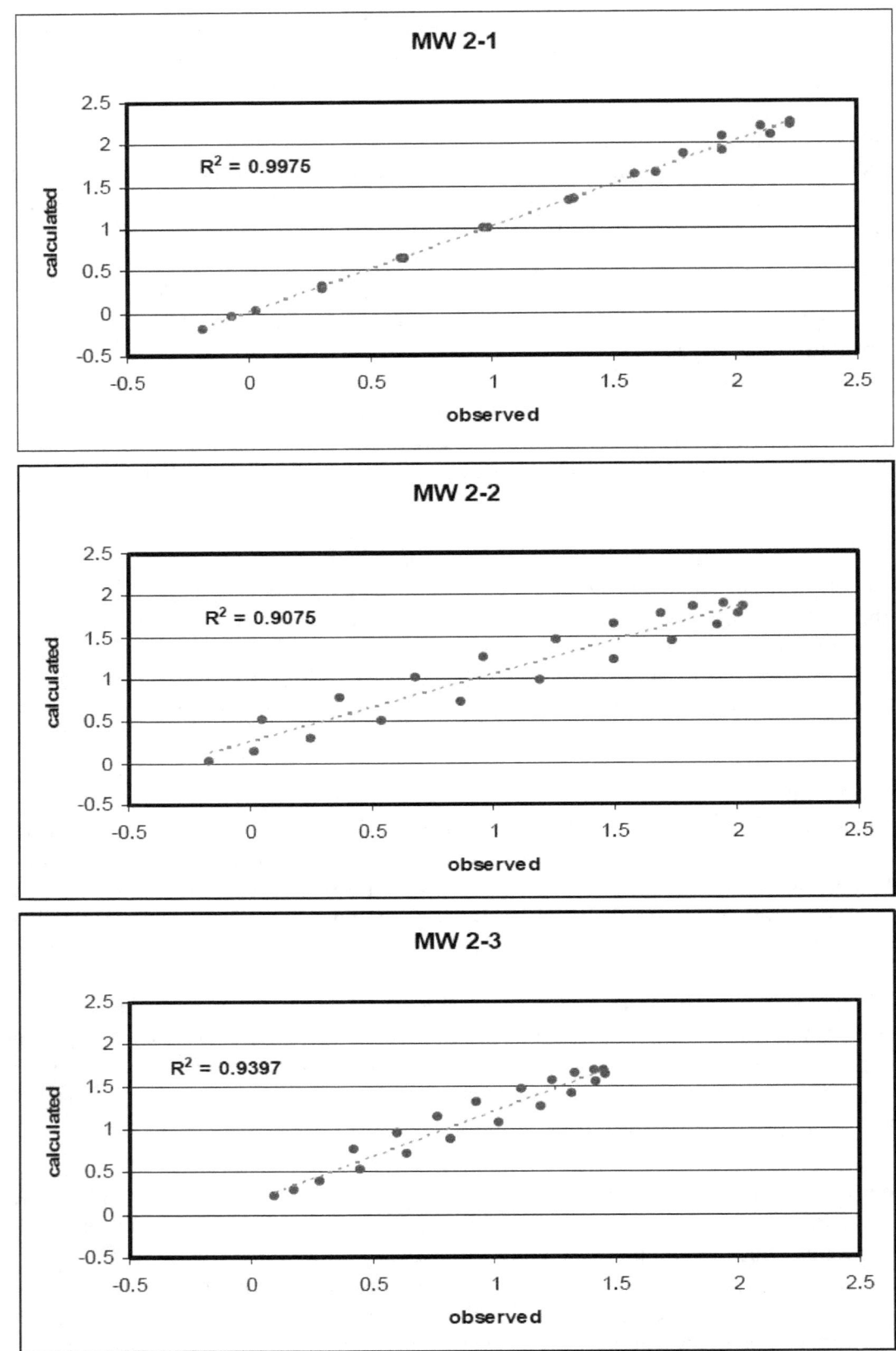

Figure 7. Correlation of observed and calculated water levels at monitoring wells.

Contour lines shown on Figures 8 and 9 represent the water table head (elevation) at one foot intervals relative to NAVD-88 (approximately mean sea level). Arrows show the direction of groundwater flow with the length of the arrow scaled to the velocity of flow. Color shading in the cross sections is correlated to the water table elevation: blue hues are -6 to -3 feet, green hues are -2 to +2 feet, and yellow to red hues are +2 to +6 feet NAVD-88 (feet above mean sea level).

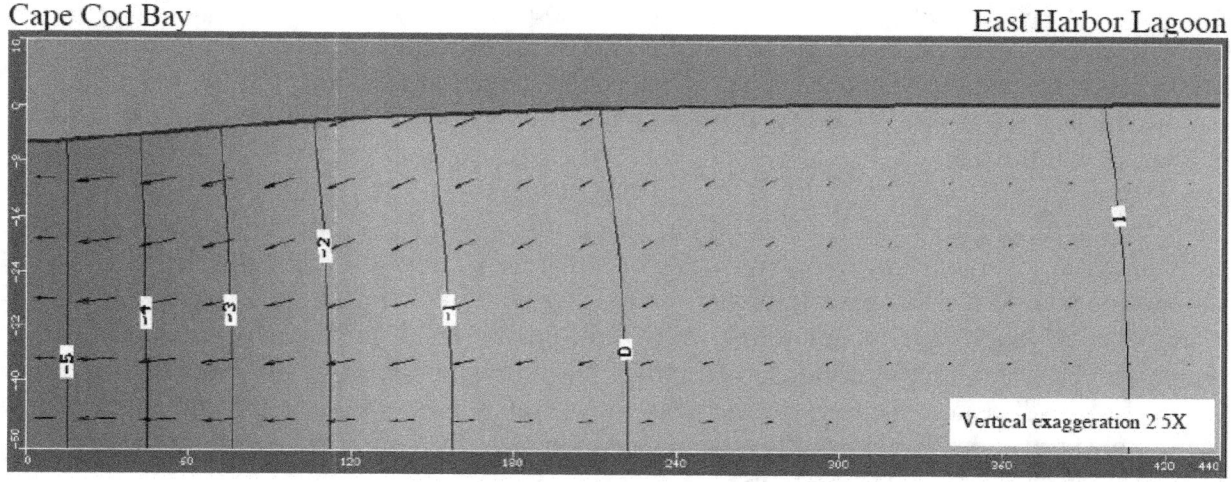

Figure 8. Cross-section through the barrier beach showing simulated groundwater flow at low tide for existing conditions (restricted tidal flow).

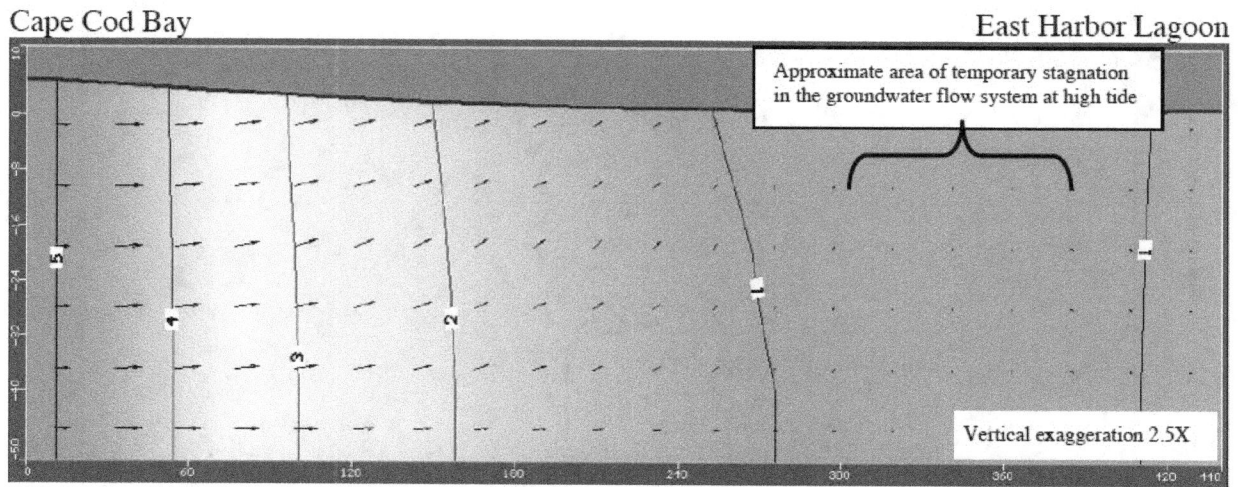

Figure 9. Cross-section through the barrier beach showing simulated groundwater flow at high tide for existing conditions (restricted tidal flow).

The model predicts that at highest monthly tides there will be short periods when the elevation of the water table in the barrier beach is higher than the water level in the lagoon (Figure 10), creating a flow gradient toward the lagoon. However, the water table gradient is low and the rate of groundwater flow toward the lagoon is very slow. As the tide begins to ebb, the water table gradient quickly reverses to again slope from the lagoon to bay.

Under current conditions, water level in the lagoon remains about 1.1 to 1.2 feet above mean sea level at all times, so even though the water table is predicted to rise to about 1.3 feet for brief periods at high tide, the low gradient and short duration of the high water table elevations preclude significant groundwater flow toward the lagoon. In the barrier beach adjacent to the lagoon, the maximum predicted gradient of the water table toward the lagoon at high tide is 0.003 ft/ft with duration of about 2 hours. The maximum predicted gradient of the water table toward the bay at low tide is 0.007 ft/ft with duration of about 8 hours during which groundwater flow is toward the bay.

The actual water table elevation in the barrier beach adjacent to the lagoon might not be higher than the water level in the lagoon. Figure 6 shows that the simulated water table elevation at monitoring well MW 2-3 (about 150 feet from the lagoon) is higher than the actual observed water table elevations in that monitoring well. If the computer model generally predicts higher than observed water table elevations in this area, it's entirely possible that the water table in the barrier beach adjacent to the lagoon is actually lower than the water level in the lagoon and that there is always (or nearly always) flow from the lagoon into the barrier beach aquifer, which ultimately discharges into Cape Cod Bay.

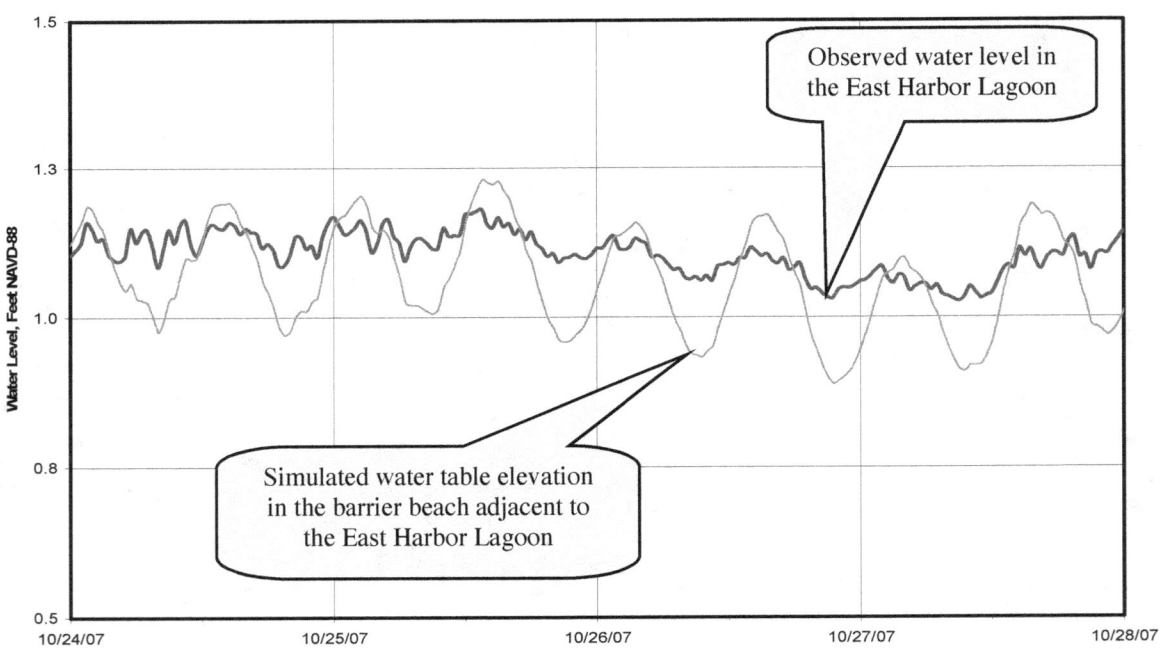

Figure 10. Comparison of simulated water table elevation in the barrier beach aquifer adjacent to the East Harbor Lagoon and observed water surface elevation in the lagoon.

The water table on the northeast half of the barrier beach, beyond 250 feet from Cape Cod Bay (the right side of the figures in this report), is nearly flat and the movement of groundwater through this part of the barrier beach is slow. Water in the East Harbor Lagoon provides a constant source of recharge for the barrier beach aquifer at an elevation of about 1.1 to 1.2 feet.

A series of cross-section plots is attached as Appendix A of this report. These plots show the progression of tidally affected groundwater levels and flow directions in the barrier beach. Water table elevations (equipotential heads) are shown by color shading and with contour lines. The arrows on the plots show the direction of groundwater flow and are scaled to the magnitude of the velocity. In many cases, the velocity is so slow that the arrow is barely perceptible and appears more as a dot than an arrow.

Particle Tracking

Particles were added to the model simulations to help visualize the potential for septic effluent to flow toward the lagoon. In all cases, regardless of where the particles were injected in the model area, the particles never discharged to the lagoon. For clarity, Figure 11 shows the track of only one particle that was injected near Rte. 6. Over a two week period, the particle moved about 75 feet toward Cape Cod Bay. Particle movement was not continuously toward the bay: there were short periods at high tide when the particle would move toward the lagoon; thus, the pattern of particle movement is five steps forward and one step back.

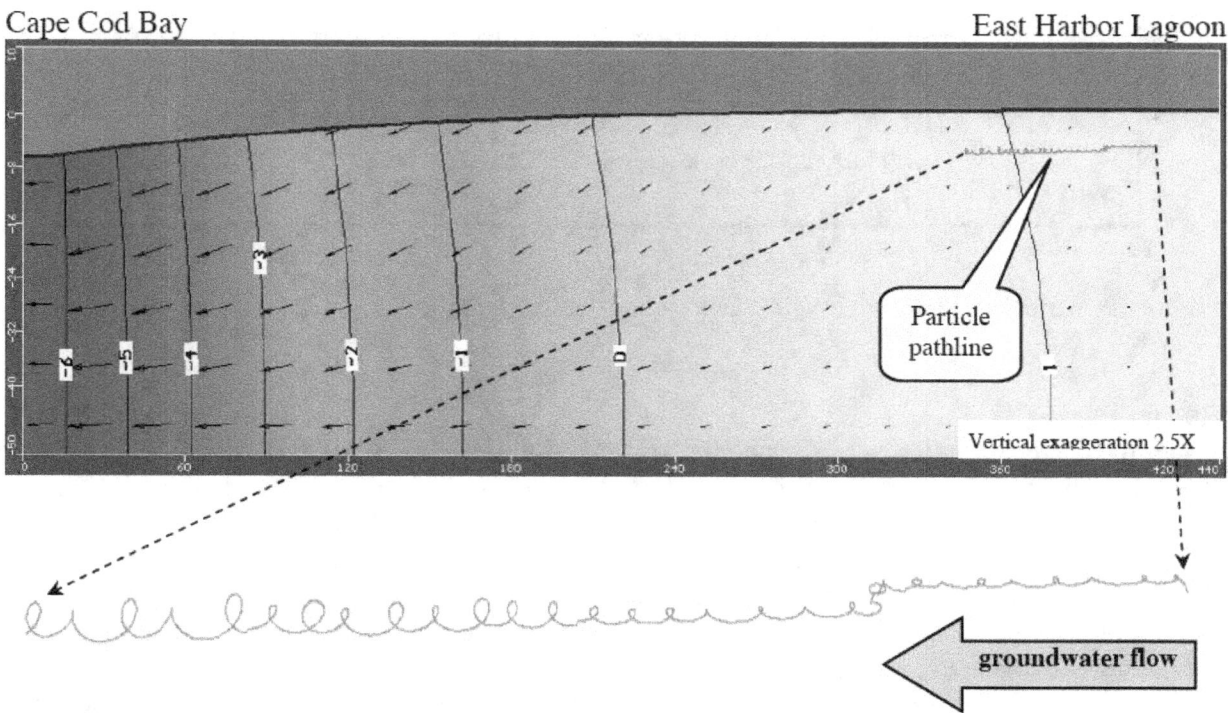

Figure 11. Particle transport toward Cape Cod Bay under current conditions
of restricted tidal flow.

Recharge Effects

A simulation was conducted with a large amount of recharge to evaluate the effect of large rainfall events on the groundwater flow system. The simulation introduced infiltration from rainfall at a rate of 2 inches/day for two days. There was very little effect on the groundwater

11

flow system. The water table rose about 0.2 feet (2½") and returned to its normal level within 6 hours of the rain stopping (Figure 12). Particle tracking was essentially unchanged.

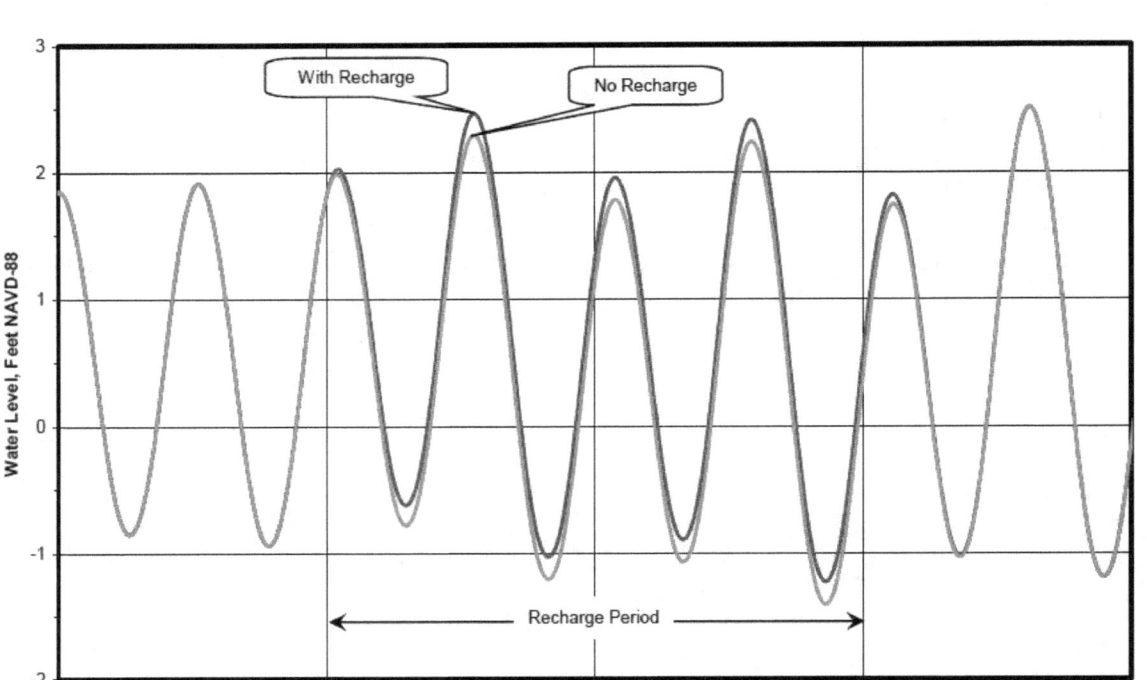

Figure 12. Effect of recharge on simulated water table elevation.

Remarks

Under the current conditions of restricted tidal flow to the East Harbor Lagoon, groundwater flow in the barrier beach between the East Harbor Lagoon and Cape Cod Bay is generally from the lagoon toward the bay. At high tide, infiltration of water from the bay causes a short duration reversal of groundwater flow in the area near the bay. Particle tracking shows no evidence for movement of nutrient-laden septic effluent toward the East Harbor Lagoon. The nearly constant water elevation in the lagoon (1.1-1.2 feet NAVD-88) provides a nearly constant head boundary for the water table in the barrier beach in the area adjacent to the lagoon. Tidal fluctuation in Cape Cod Bay causes tidal fluctuation of the water table in the barrier beach adjacent to the bay.

Groundwater Flow - Restored Tidal Flow to East Harbor

Spaulding and Grilli (2005) modeled tidal flow in the East Harbor Lagoon for various sizes and configurations of tide control structures and openings through the barrier beach separating the lagoon from Cape Cod Bay. Two of their modeled scenarios for restored tidal flow (50-meter wide inlet and 100-meter wide inlet) were selected for analyses using the MODFLOW groundwater model to assess the probable effects of tidal restoration on groundwater flow and water table fluctuations within the barrier beach. The primary objective of this modeling was to determine whether restoration of tidal flow to the East Harbor Lagoon would create a set of conditions that could cause septic effluent, or other contaminants, to flow from developed areas on Beach Point toward the lagoon.

Predicted Tidal Fluctuation

The two tidal conditions that are evaluated with the MODFLOW model are Spaulding's "R1-1C" and "R1-2C". Condition R1-1C is a 50-meter wide inlet with a bottom elevation at -1 meter NAVD-88 (one meter below sea level). Condition R1-2C is a 100-meter wide inlet with a bottom elevation at -1 meter NAVD-88.

There is only one parcel of undeveloped public land (Noons Landing) along the barrier beach separating the lagoon from the bay that could accommodate a 50-meter wide inlet structure. Thus, a 50-meter wide inlet likely represents the maximum tidal restoration possible with existing development of the barrier beach. A 100-meter wide inlet was also evaluated to test the system with a much wider opening and predicted tidal range, despite the practical constraints of modern barrier-beach development.

The tidal modeling of Spaulding and Grilli (2005) generated a dataset for one tidal cycle for each scenario evaluated. The dataset for each scenario contains tide levels in Cape Cod Bay and the East Harbor Lagoon at 15-minute intervals for 13 hours (Fig. 13). Evaluation of the effects of various tidal conditions on groundwater flow in the barrier beach requires running the MODFLOW model with a given set of conditions for several days to allow groundwater in the barrier beach to equilibrate to the specified tidal conditions. Therefore, the datasets were extended by repeating the predicted tidal fluctuations to extend them from one tide cycle to ten days. An example of the extended dataset for several tide cycles is shown in Figure 13.

The size of the open area of a tide control structure restricts the flow of water between the bay and the lagoon. High tide in the East Harbor Lagoon lags behind high tide in Cape Cod Bay by about half an hour for a 100-meter wide inlet and 1¼ hours for a 50-meter wide inlet. Maintaining an artificial base elevation of -1 meter at the tidal inlet structures affects water levels in the lagoon by restricting outflow of water from the lagoon during the falling tide. As the tide in Cape Cod Bay is beginning to recede, the water level in the bay is still higher than in the lagoon. Water continues to flow into the lagoon and the water level in the lagoon continues to rise until the receding tide in the bay is lower than the water level in the lagoon and water begins to flow out of the lagoon. Drainage of water from the lagoon (and the low tide level in the lagoon) is restricted by the bottom elevation of the inlet structure, -1 meter in this case. As water levels in the lagoon fall, the gradient decreases and the outflow from the lagoon decreases. Low tide in the lagoon is about 1 foot below sea level for a 50-meter wide inlet and occurs about 2¾ hours after low tide in the bay. Low tide in the lagoon is about 2.5 feet below sea level for a 100-meter wide inlet and occurs about 2¼ hours after low tide in the bay. For comparison, low tide in the bay is 6 feet below sea level. Lag times and water levels for tidal fluctuation are shown in Figure 13 and summarized in Table 1.

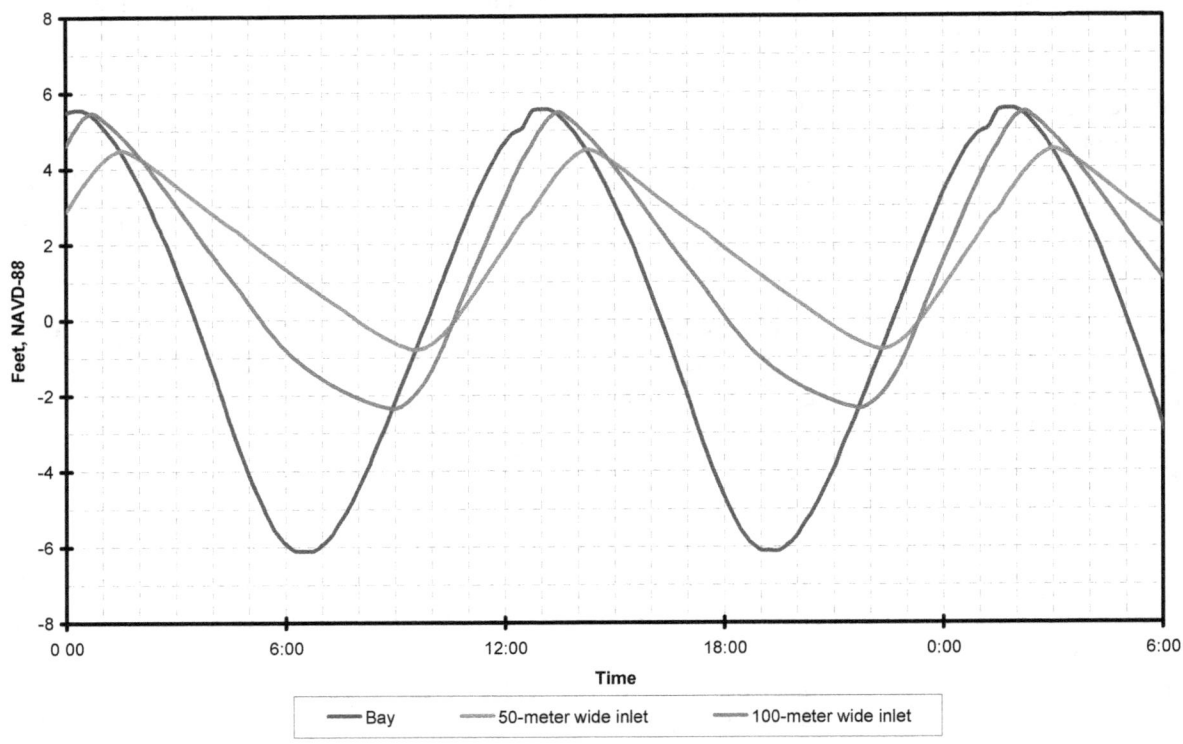

Figure 13. Predicted tidal fluctuation in the East Harbor Lagoon for two tidal inlet structures.

Table 1. Model-predicted ebb- and flood-tide durations, high- and low-tide elevations (NAVD88), and tidal delays between Cape Cod Bay and the East Harbor Lagoon.

	Cape Cod Bay	East Harbor Lagoon	
		50-meter wide inlet	100-meter wide inlet
Delay from high tide in the bay to high tide in the lagoon	----	1¼ hours	½ hour
Delay from low tide in the bay to low tide in the lagoon	----	2¾ hours	2¼ hours
Duration of rising tide	6¼ hours	4¾ hours	4½ hours
Duration of falling tide	6½ hours	8 hours	8¼ hours
Elevation of high tide	5.6 feet	4.5 feet	5.5 feet
Elevation of low tide	-6.1 feet	-0.8 feet	-2.3 feet

Predicted Effects on Groundwater Flow in the Barrier Beach

Groundwater flow in the barrier beach was simulated for 10 days using the MODFLOW model. A dataset for fluctuating tide levels in Cape Cod Bay and the East Harbor Lagoon was generated by repeating the dataset of Spaulding and Grilli until the data covered a 10-day period. These data were used to define transient boundary conditions at the shoreline of both the bay and lagoon.

Groundwater elevations and flow equilibrated to the new tidal regime within a day or two. After that, water table elevations and groundwater flow at any point within the barrier beach varied with the same regularity as the tidal fluctuation; i.e., conditions at any particular location in the barrier beach were the same at 2 hours after high tide on day 4, day 5,....and day 10. The resultant data and particle tracking from the MODFLOW model could be used to predict the groundwater flow regime within the barrier beach for the anticipated tidal regimes following restoration of tidal flow to the lagoon.

Figures 14 through 21 show a series of cross sections through the barrier beach at high and low tides in Cape Cod Bay and the East Harbor Lagoon for two different tidal inlet structures (50 & 100 meter wide openings). Elevation contours in these figures show the water table elevation in feet NAVD-88. Arrows show the direction of groundwater flow with the length of the arrow scaled to the velocity of flow. Color shading in the cross sections is correlated to the water table elevation: blue hues are -6 to -3 feet, green hues are -2 to +2 feet, and yellow to red hues are +2 to +6 feet NAVD-88 (approximately feet above mean sea level).

High Tide

Figures 14 and 15 depict groundwater flow in a cross-section through the barrier beach at high tide in the bay and lagoon for a 50-meter wide inlet. Figures 16 and 17 depict groundwater flow in a cross-section through the barrier beach at high tide in the bay and lagoon for a 100-meter wide inlet.

Figures 14 and 16 show groundwater flow conditions in the barrier beach at high tide in Cape Cod Bay. Water from the bay and lagoon is infiltrating into the barrier beach, causing the water table to rise in the near shore areas, and to a lesser extent in the middle part of the beach. As the tide in the bay begins to recede, the tide in the lagoon continues to rise because the water level in the lagoon is still lower than the water level in the bay. The water level in the lagoon continues to rise for about 1¼ hours after high tide in the bay for a 50-meter wide inlet and ½ hour for a 100-meter wide inlet. During this time water continues to infiltrate the barrier beach from the lagoon side and the water table near the lagoon continues to rise, while at the same time the water table is declining on the bay side of the barrier beach.

Figures 15 and 17 show groundwater flow in the barrier beach at the time of the highest tidal elevation in the East Harbor Lagoon, about 1¼ hours after the tide in Cape Cod Bay started to recede for a 50-meter wide inlet and ½ hour for a 100-meter wide inlet. Groundwater flow patterns in the barrier beach at high tide for both conditions R1-1C and R1-2C look very similar. (Compare Figures 14 and 15 to Figures 16 and 17.) Water table elevations on the bay side of the barrier beach are identical at the time of high tide for both conditions (Figures 14 and 16) because the tidal regime for the bay is identical for both conditions. The difference in water table elevations in the barrier beach adjacent to the bay at the occurrence of high tide in the lagoon (Figures 15 and 17) is simply due to a difference in elapsed time after high tide in the bay (1¼ hours in Figure 15 and ½ hours in Figure 17). The water table on the lagoon side of the barrier beach is higher (and the rise occurs earlier) for a 100-meter wide inlet because in this case the high tide elevation in the lagoon is nearly the same as in the bay, as shown on Figure 14.

The time of occurrence and the elevation of high tides in the lagoon for a 100-meter wide inlet more closely approximate Cape Cod Bay because the wider inlet is less of a restriction to inflow. The lag time between high tides in the bay and lagoon is only about ½ hour for a 100-meter wide inlet vs. 1¼ hours for a 50-meter wide inlet (Figure 14).

Low Tide
Figures 18 and 19 depict groundwater flow in a cross-section through the barrier beach at low tide in the bay and lagoon for a 50-meter wide inlet. Figures 20 and 21 depict groundwater flow in a cross-section through the barrier beach at low tide in the bay and lagoon for a 100-meter wide inlet.

Figures 18 and 20 show groundwater flow conditions in the barrier beach at low tide in Cape Cod Bay. Water from most of the barrier beach is flowing toward and discharging to the bay because the water level in the bay is much lower than the water table elevation in the lagoon. There is very little flow between the barrier beach and the lagoon for a 50-meter wide inlet because the water surface elevation in the lagoon is nearly the same as the water table elevation in the barrier beach adjacent to the lagoon. The base elevation of the tidal inlet structure (-1 meter) and the narrow opening (50 meters) impede outflow of water from the lagoon during the receding part of the tide cycle. There is more groundwater flow from the barrier beach to the lagoon for a 100-meter wide inlet (Figure 20) because the larger opening in the tide control structure allows more water to drain from the lagoon, resulting in lower water-surface elevations at low tide.

Low tide occurs in the East Harbor Lagoon approximately 2¾ hours after low tide in the bay for a 50-meter wide inlet. During the time between low tide in the bay and low tide in the lagoon, groundwater continually flows from the lagoon side toward the bay side of the barrier beach. Thereafter, as the water level of the lagoon continues to recede, groundwater flows toward and discharges to the lagoon. . Flow toward the lagoon is less than toward the bay because the water table gradient toward the lagoon is lower. At the time of low tide in the lagoon, the tide in the bay has been rising for several hours and water has been infiltrating the barrier beach adjacent to the bay, causing the water table near the bay to rise (Figure 19).

Cross sections at low tide for both 50-meter and 100-meter inlet conditions look very similar. (Compare Figures 18 and 19 to Figures 20 and 21.) Water table elevations on the bay side of the barrier beach are identical at the time of low tide in the bay (Figures 18 and 20) because the tidal regime for the bay is identical for both simulations. The water table on the lagoon side of the barrier beach is lower for a 100-meter wide inlet because the low tide elevation in the lagoon is less than for a 50-meter wide inlet, as shown on Figure 14.

Figure 21 shows that for a 100-meter wide inlet there is considerably more groundwater flow toward and discharge to the lagoon (at the time of low tide in the lagoon) than for a 50-meter wide inlet. Compare Figures 19 and 21 to see the differences in water table elevation, direction of groundwater flow, and velocity for the two conditions. Although there is more movement of groundwater toward, and discharge to, the lagoon at low tide for a 100-meter wide inlet, the net flow of groundwater in the barrier beach is still toward Cape Cod Bay. The inflow of water from the lagoon to the barrier beach at high tide exceeds the return flow of groundwater to the lagoon at low tide. Thus, the net flow of groundwater was from the lagoon, into the barrier beach, and toward the bay. Computer simulations of groundwater flow always showed net groundwater flow from the developed area of Beach Point toward Cape Cod Bay.

Remarks
Observations and analyses of output from the MODFLOW model verify what should be intuitively obvious from analyses of the hydrographs of tidal fluctuation (Figure 14). The wider tidal inlet (100 vs. 50 meters) is less of a restriction to tidal flow and allows the high tide conditions in the lagoon to more closely approximate the bay.

Constructing the bottom elevation of the tide control structures at -1 meter NAVD-88 restricts outflow from the lagoon, maintaining the low-tide elevation in the lagoon at a higher elevation and delaying low tide. Higher water elevations in the lagoon at low tide maintain higher water table elevations in the groundwater system on the lagoon side of the barrier beach. Therefore, throughout the low-tide period, less groundwater flows toward the lagoon than toward the bay, reducing the potential for septic effluent and other contaminants to flow from the developed parts of the barrier beach toward the lagoon.

Cape Cod Bay   East Harbor Lagoon

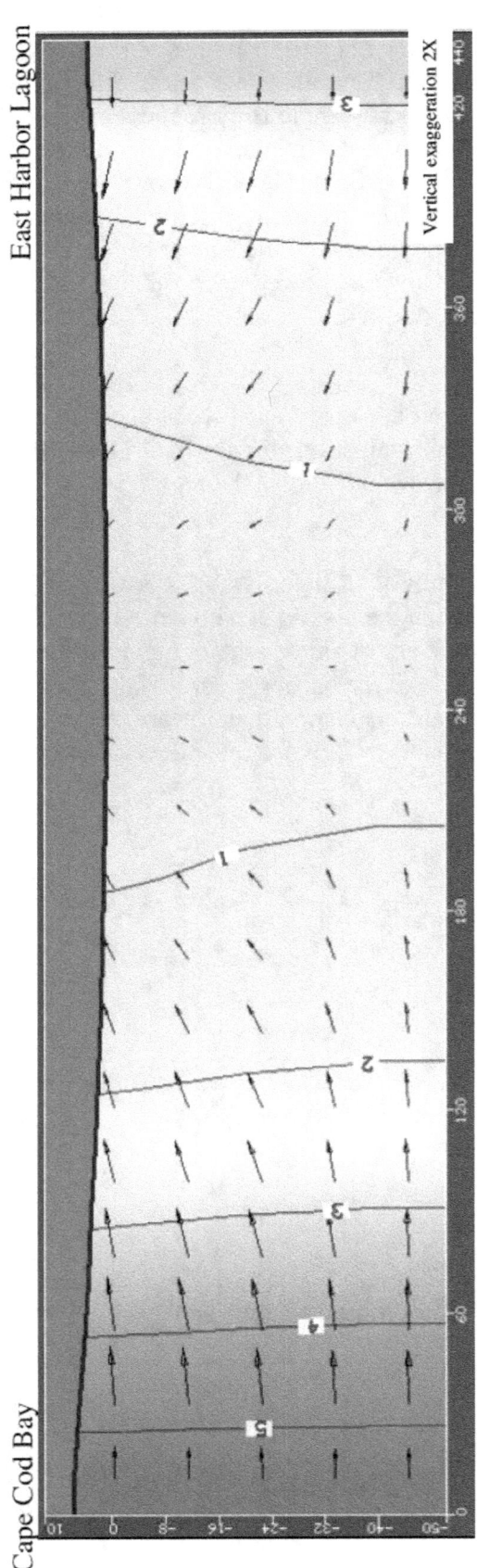

Figure 14. Cross-section through the barrier beach showing groundwater flow at high tide in Cape Cod Bay, 50-meter wide inlet.

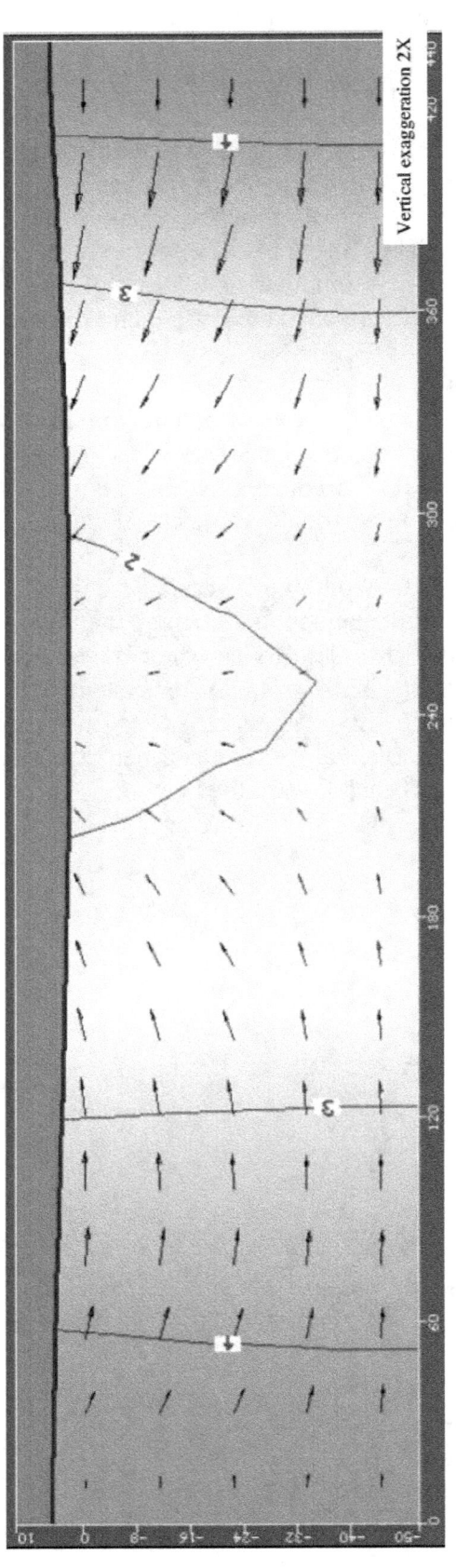

Figure 15. Cross-section through the barrier beach showing groundwater flow at high tide in the East Harbor Lagoon, 50-meter wide inlet, 1¼ hours after high tide in Cape Cod Bay.

18

Cape Cod Bay   East Harbor Lagoon

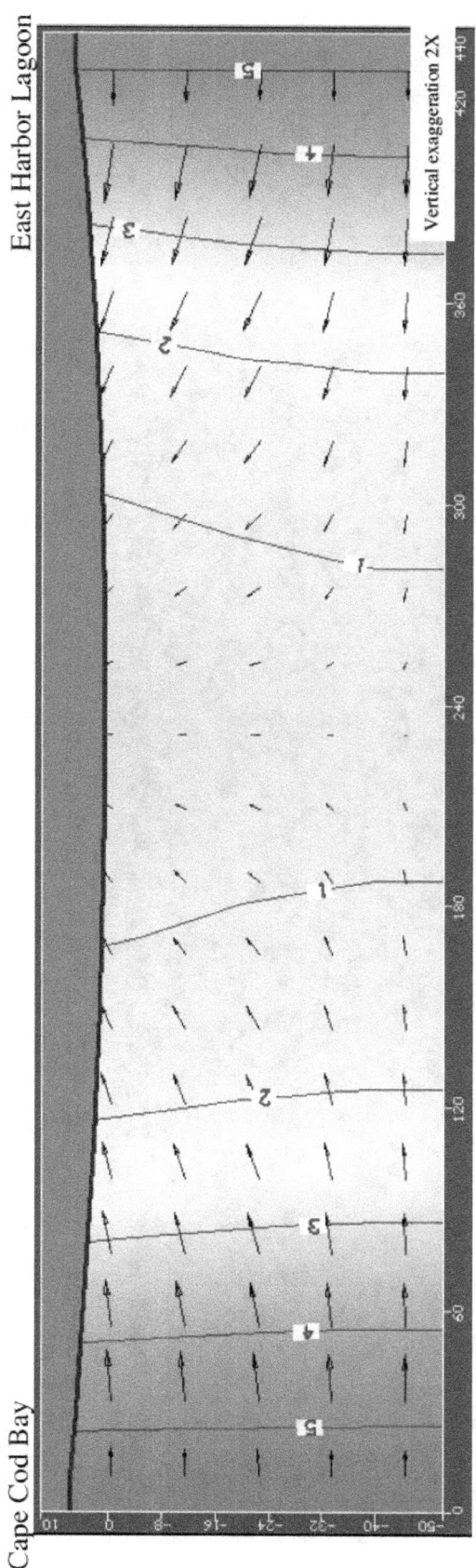

Figure 16. Cross-section through the barrier beach showing groundwater flow at high tide in Cape Cod Bay, 100-meter wide inlet.

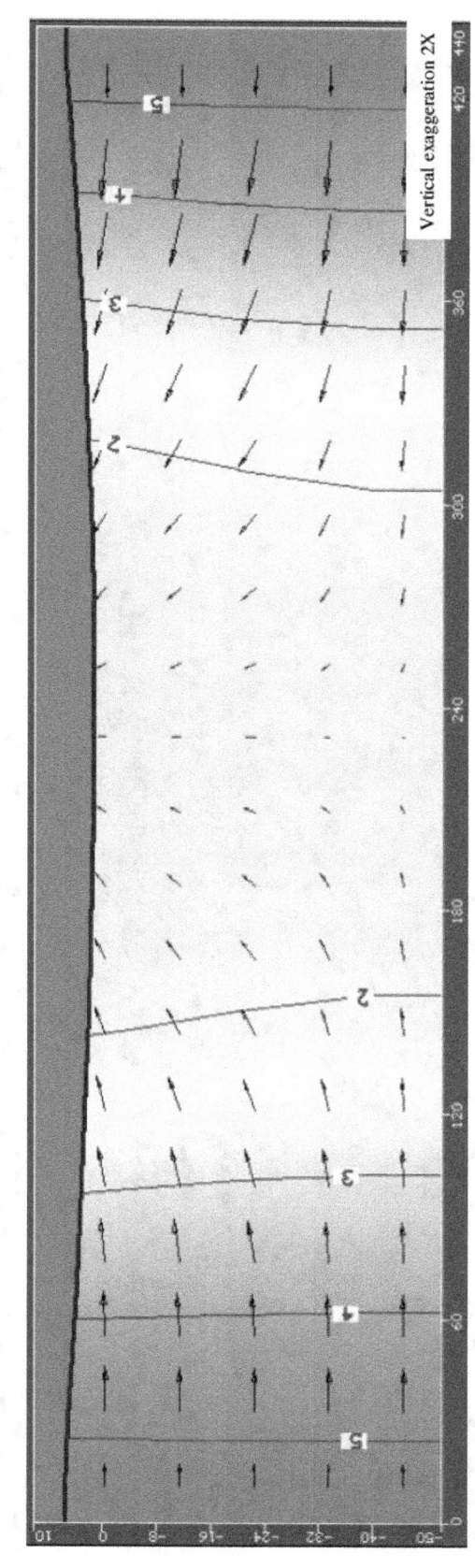

Figure 17. Cross-section through the barrier beach showing groundwater flow at high tide in the East Harbor Lagoon, 100-meter wide inlet, ½ hour after high tide in Cape Cod Bay.

19

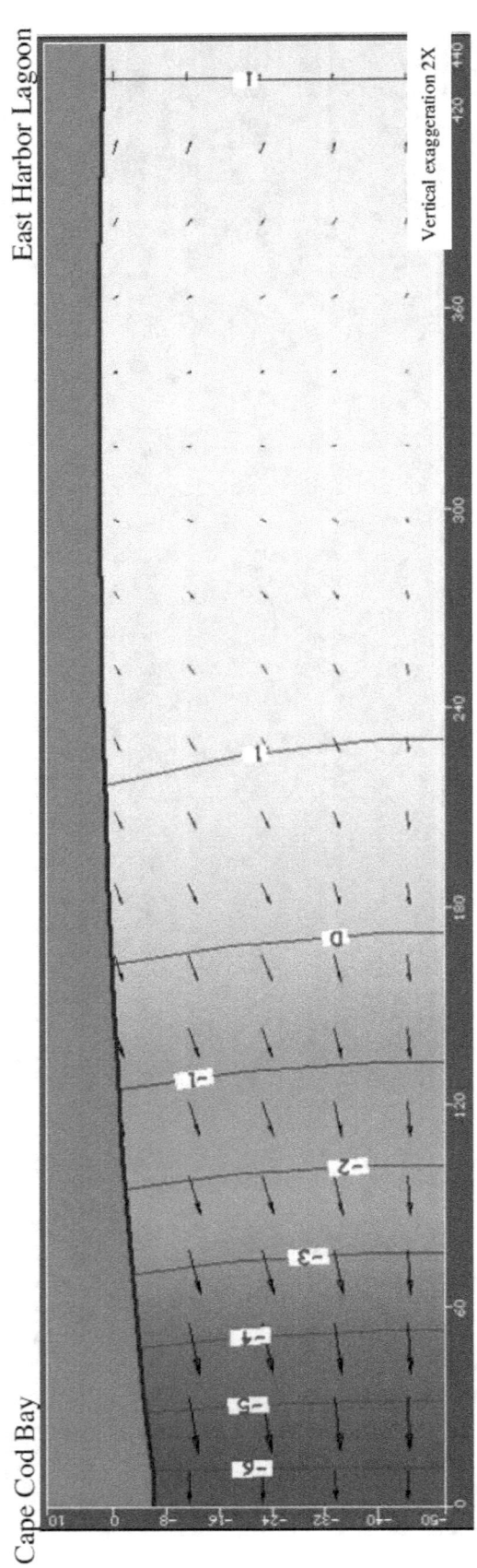

Figure 18. Cross-section through the barrier beach showing groundwater flow at low tide in Cape Cod Bay, 50-meter wide inlet.

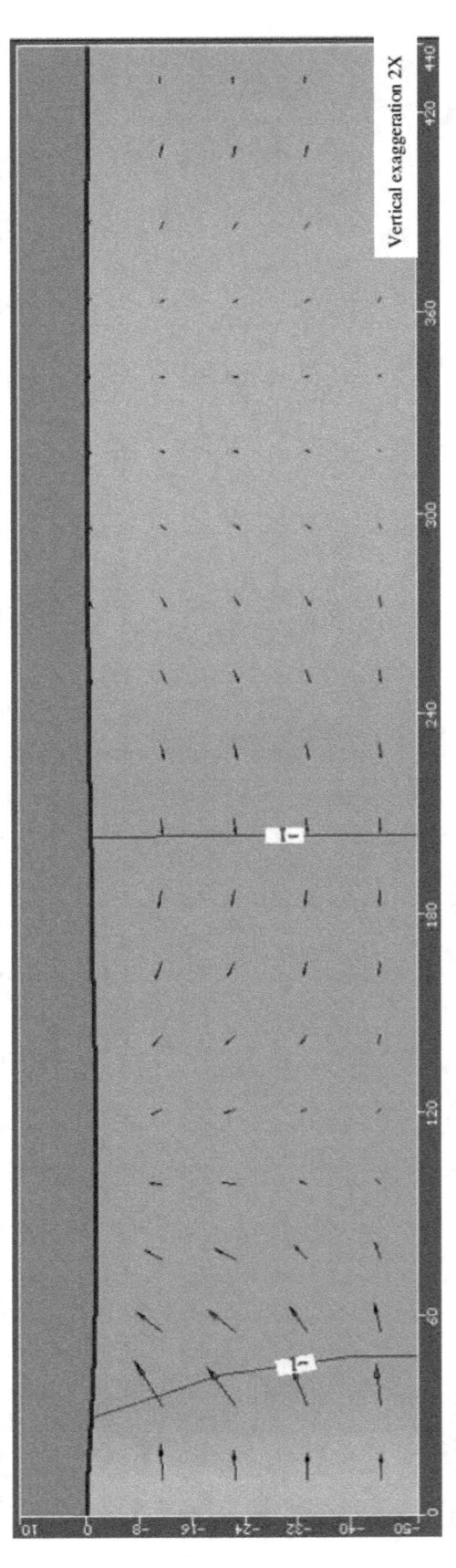

Figure 19. Cross-section through the barrier beach showing groundwater flow at low tide in the East Harbor Lagoon, 50-meter wide inlet, 2¾ hours after low tide in Cape Cod Bay.

20

Cape Cod Bay   East Harbor Lagoon

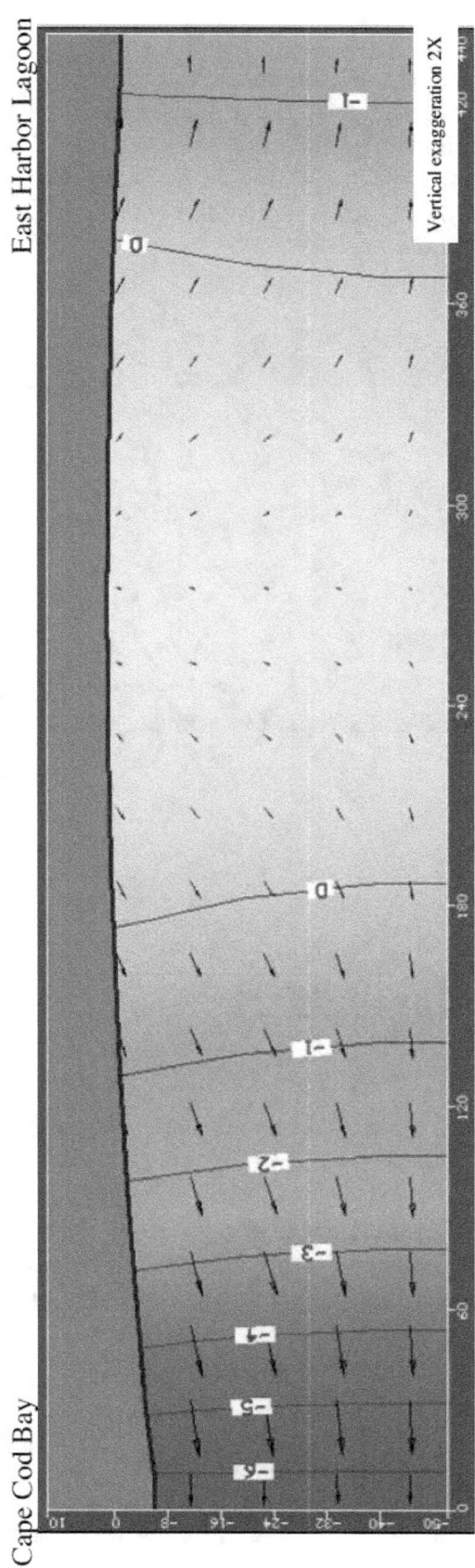

Figure 20. Cross-section through the barrier beach showing groundwater flow at low tide in Cape Cod Bay, 100-meter wide inlet.

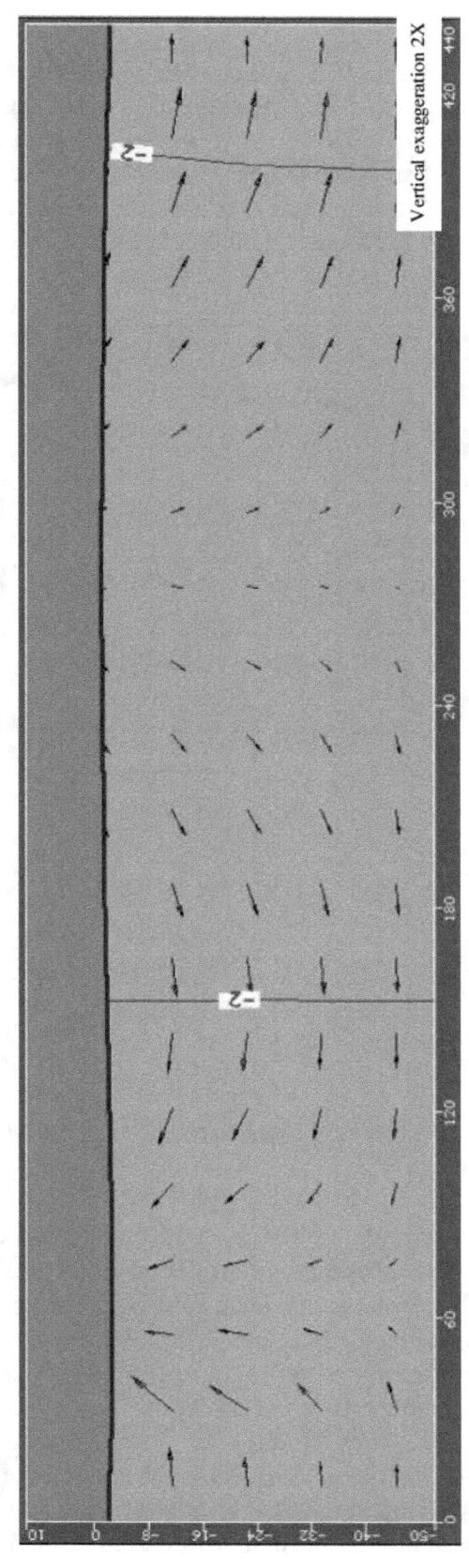

Figure 21. Cross-section through the barrier beach showing groundwater flow at low tide in the East Harbor Lagoon, 100-meter wide inlet, 2¼ hours after low tide in Cape Cod Bay.

21

Particle Tracking

Additional MODFLOW simulations were made using the same tidal conditions, but adding a series of particles to allow visualization of the movement of groundwater. Particles were released to the groundwater system throughout the model domain. All particles showed a surging, or pulsing, movement correlated to the tidal regime. For clarity, Figure 22 shows the pathline of a single particle that was released 25 feet from the lagoon in the MODFLOW simulation for a 50-meter wide inlet.

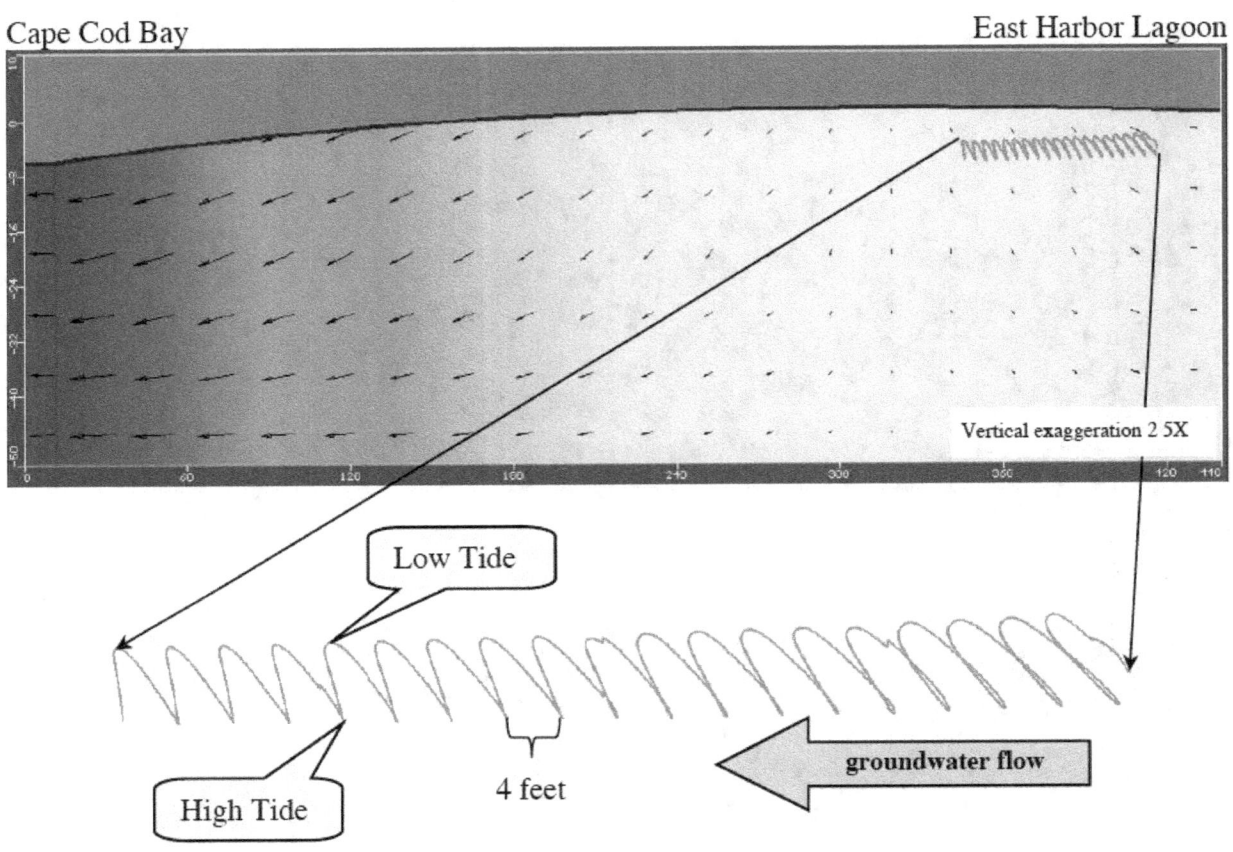

Figure 22. Pathline of a particle released in the MODFLOW simulation of a 50-meter wide inlet.

Particle tracking shows that the net flow of groundwater is toward Cape Cod Bay. At low tide there is greater movement of groundwater toward Cape Cod Bay, and at high tide there is a lesser flow of groundwater toward the East Harbor Lagoon. The net flow of groundwater for all tidal conditions, and at all locations within the barrier beach, was toward Cape Cod Bay. The net movement of groundwater in this example (50-meter wide inlet) is about 4 feet toward the bay with each complete tidal cycle (i.e., from one low tide to the next low tide).

Figure 23 shows the pathline for a particle released 25 feet from the lagoon during the MODFLOW simulation of a 100-meter wide inlet. Low tide elevation in the lagoon for a 100-meter wide inlet is lower than for a 50-meter wide inlet. Thus, there is more groundwater flow

22

toward the lagoon at low tide. Nevertheless, the net flow of groundwater remains toward Cape Cod Bay for all locations within the barrier beach. The net movement of groundwater in this example (100-meter wide inlet) is about 2½ feet toward the bay with each complete tidal cycle (i.e., from one low tide to the next low tide).

Cape Cod Bay   East Harbor Lagoon

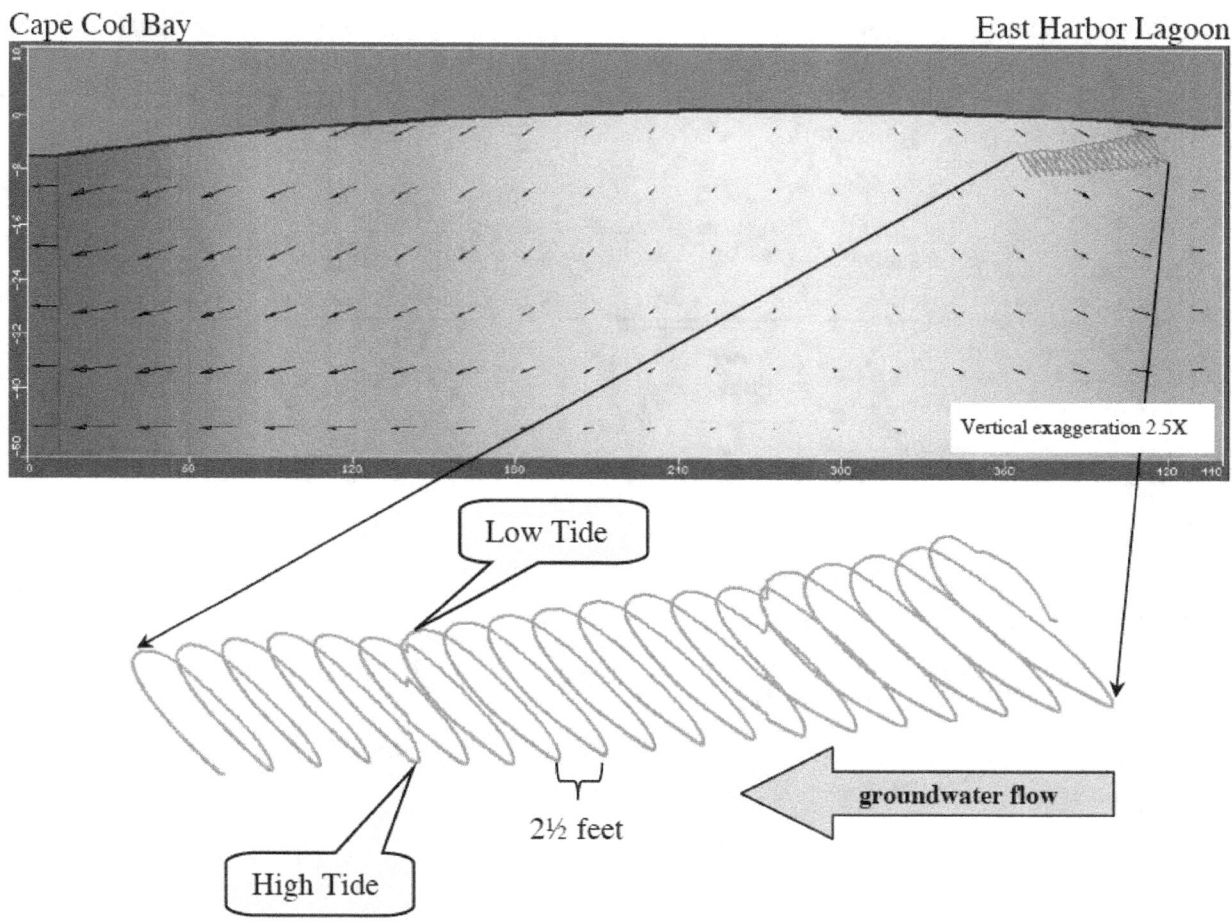

Figure 23. Pathline of a particle released in the MODFLOW simulation of a 100-meter wide inlet.

Effect of Recharge from a Septic Leachfield

Additional simulations were conducted to simulate the effects of recharge to the groundwater system by effluent from a septic leachfield. A recharge rate of 10,000 gpd (gallons per day) for a single cell (20 ft x 100 ft) in the model was used to simulate the potential effects of inflow from a larger occupancy development. The recharge was modeled to occur in the cell immediately to the northeast of Rte. 6A, under the presumption that would be a likely location for a leachfield that would be large enough to handle the effluent from a multiple occupancy development. Although 10,000 gpd seems like a lot of water, it is an average of only 7 gallons per minute over an entire day and is spread over an area of 2000 ft^2.

The following example shows the simulated effects for a 50-meter wide inlet with the bottom elevation of the tide control structure at -1 meter (NAVD88). Results for simulation of recharge from septic effluent for a 100-meter wide inlet are nearly identical and therefore not shown here.

The maximum water table elevation change would be expected to occur in the middle of the cell, where the recharge occurs. The water table is predicted to rise ¾ inch in response to the simulated influx of septic effluent (Figure 24). The water table fluctuation due to tidal effects is about 4 feet. The inflow of water from recharge is quickly transmitted to adjacent areas through the porous sand that comprises the barrier beach. The sand is too porous to allow significant mounding of groundwater in the recharge area. Changing the water table elevation by ¾ inch is unlikely to have a perceptible effect on groundwater flow in comparison with the 4 feet of fluctuation that occurs with each tide cycle.

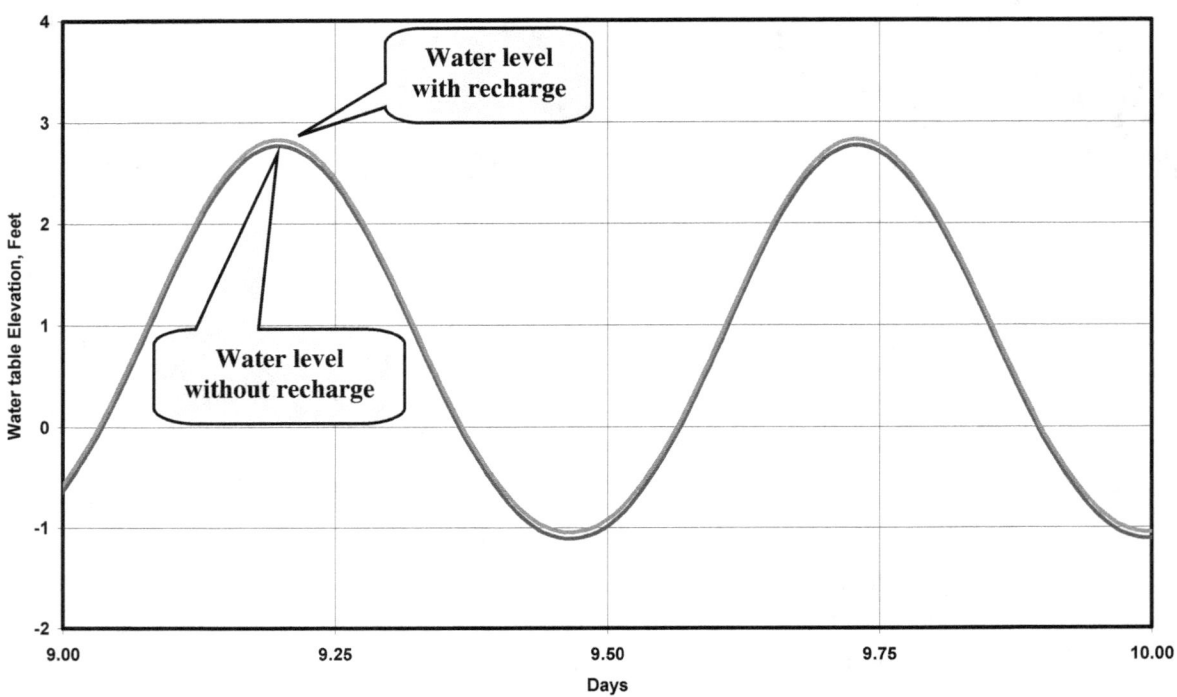

Figure 24. Simulated water table elevation in an area of the groundwater flow model having a recharge rate of 10,000 gpd. Tidal restoration with a 50-meter wide inlet. Results for a 100-meter wide inlet are nearly identical.

Figure 25 shows the predicted flowpath for a particle released in a septic leachfield in the developed area adjacent to Rte. 6A. The flowpath is nearly identical to the previous examples, showing the cyclic to-and-fro motion caused by tidal fluctuation. It appears that the effect of tidal fluctuations overwhelms any effect of recharge from on-site sewage disposal systems.

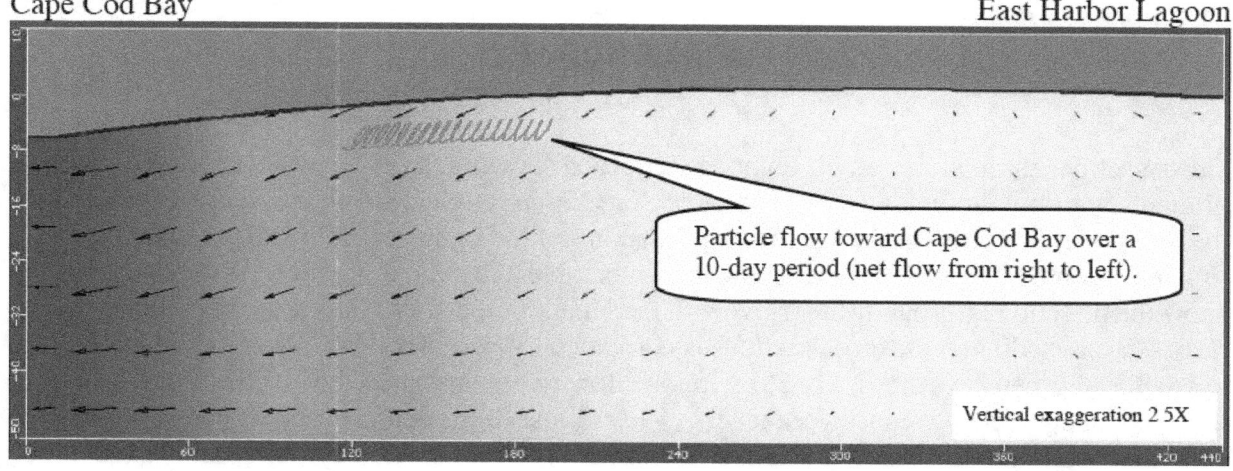

Figure 25. Pathline for a particle released in a cell having a recharge rate of 10,000 gpd.

Conclusions

Groundwater flow in the barrier beach separating the East Harbor Lagoon from Cape Cod Bay was simulated using the MODFLOW computer model. Simulations were conducted for existing tide-restricted and proposed tide-restoration regimes in the East Harbor Lagoon. Results show that the net flow of groundwater is always toward Cape Cod Bay for all simulated conditions. Septic effluent and any other contaminants that might be introduced to the groundwater system in the developed area of Beach Point along Rte. 6A will always flow toward, and discharge to, Cape Cod Bay.

Literature Cited

Spaulding, M. and A. Grilli, 2005, *Hydrodynamic assessment of estuarine restoration of Pilgrim Lake, Moon Pond, and Salt Meadow, Truro, Massachusetts*, unpublished Report to National Park Service, 45 pp.

Appendix A

Cross-sections through the Beach Point barrier beach showing the effect of tidal fluctuation on groundwater flow through a complete tide cycle. Cross-sections extend from Cape Cod Bay (on the left of the diagrams) to the East Harbor Lagoon (on the right side of the diagrams). Elevation contours in these figures show the water table elevation in feet NAVD-88. Arrows show the direction of groundwater flow with the length of the arrow scaled to the velocity of flow. Color shading in the cross sections is correlated to the water table elevation; blue hues are -6 to -3 feet, green hues are -2 to +2 feet, and yellow to red hues are +2 to +6 feet NAVD-88 (approximately feet above mean sea level). The cross-sections depict groundwater flow for existing conditions with restricted tidal flow between the lagoon and bay. Vertical exaggeration in these figures is 2X.

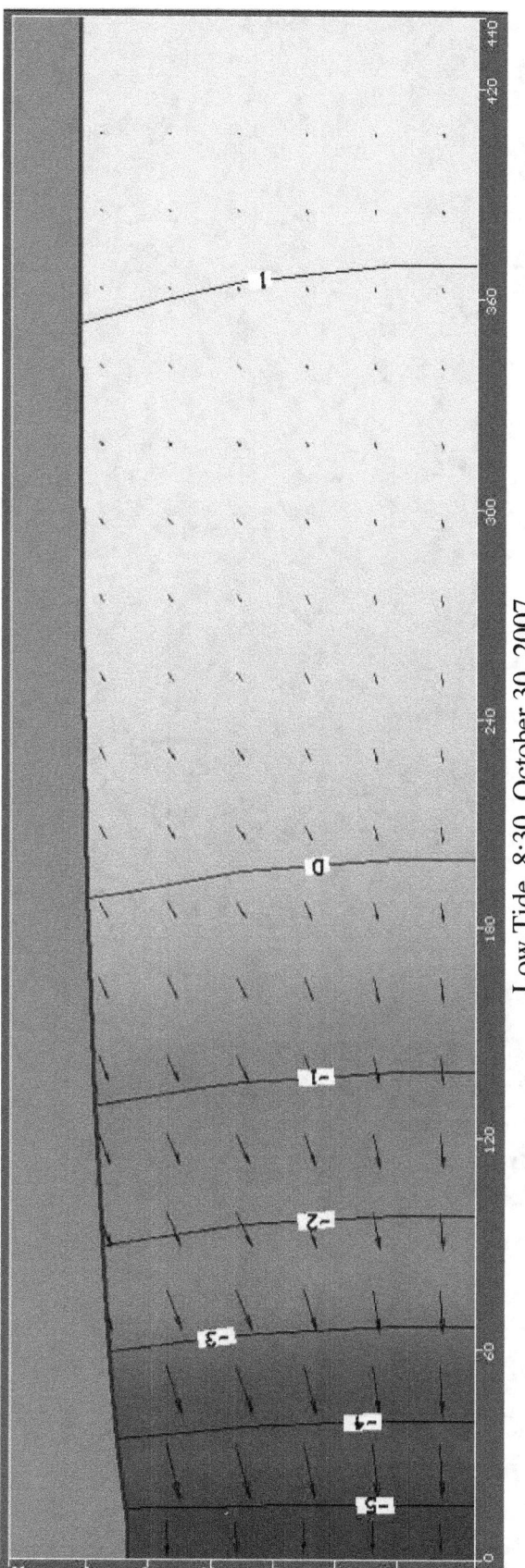

Low Tide, 8:30, October 30, 2007

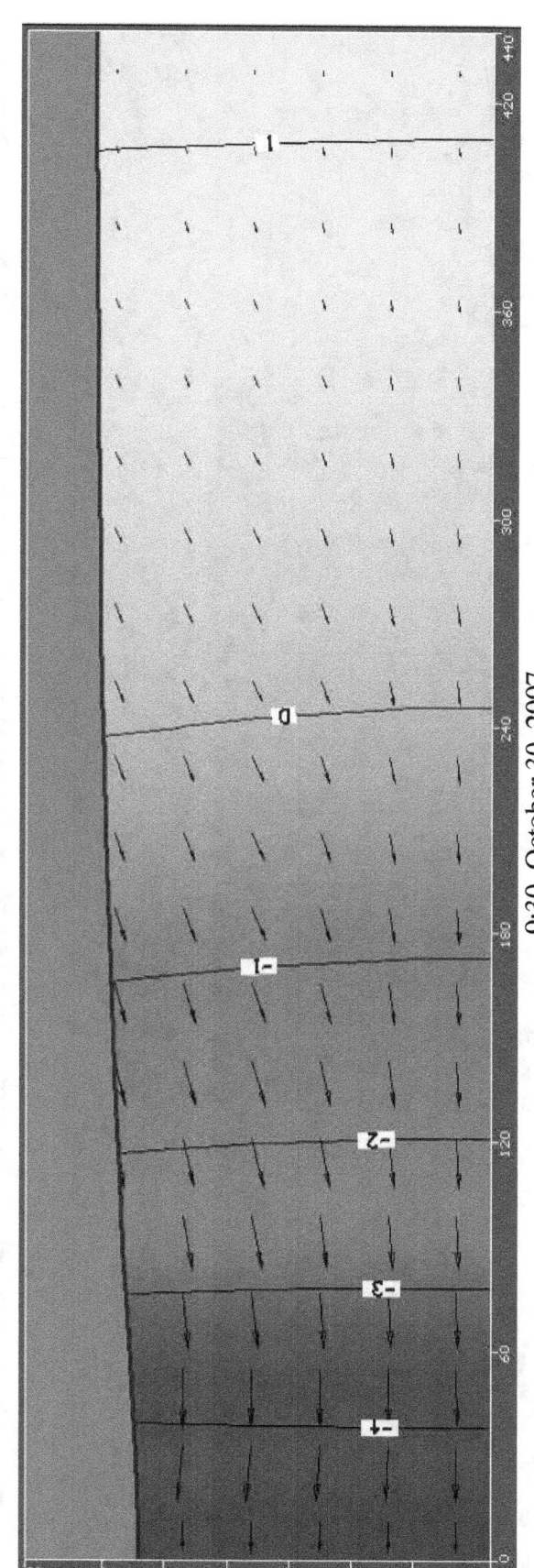

9:30, October 30, 2007

27

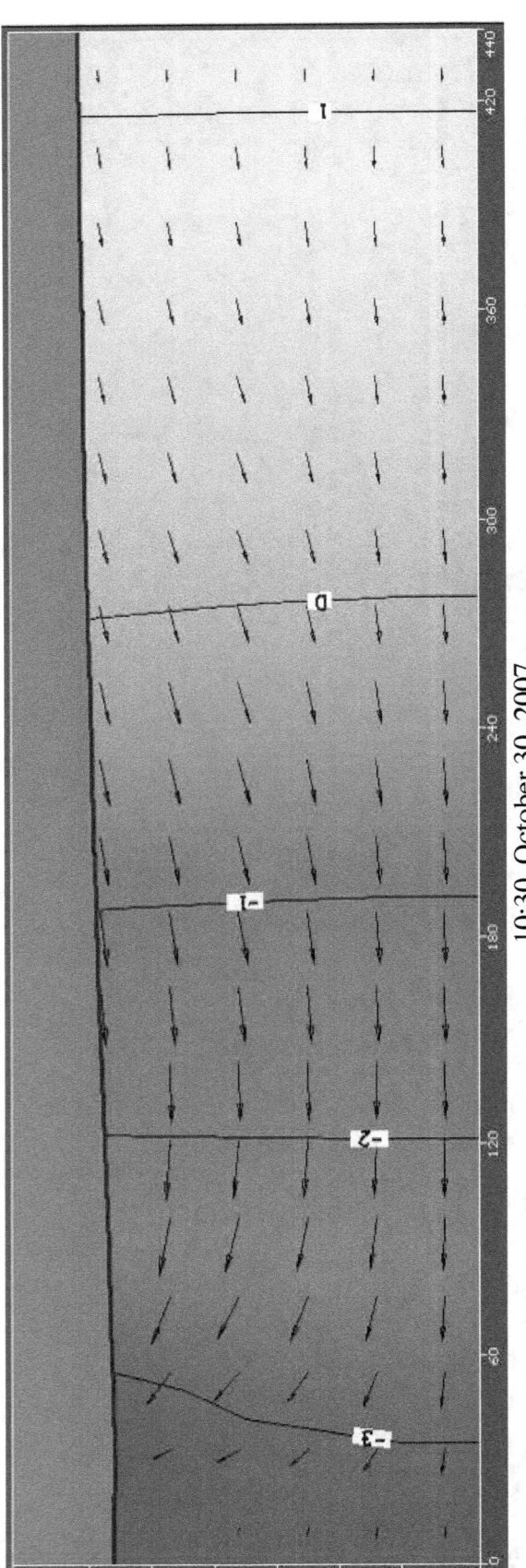

10:30, October 30, 2007

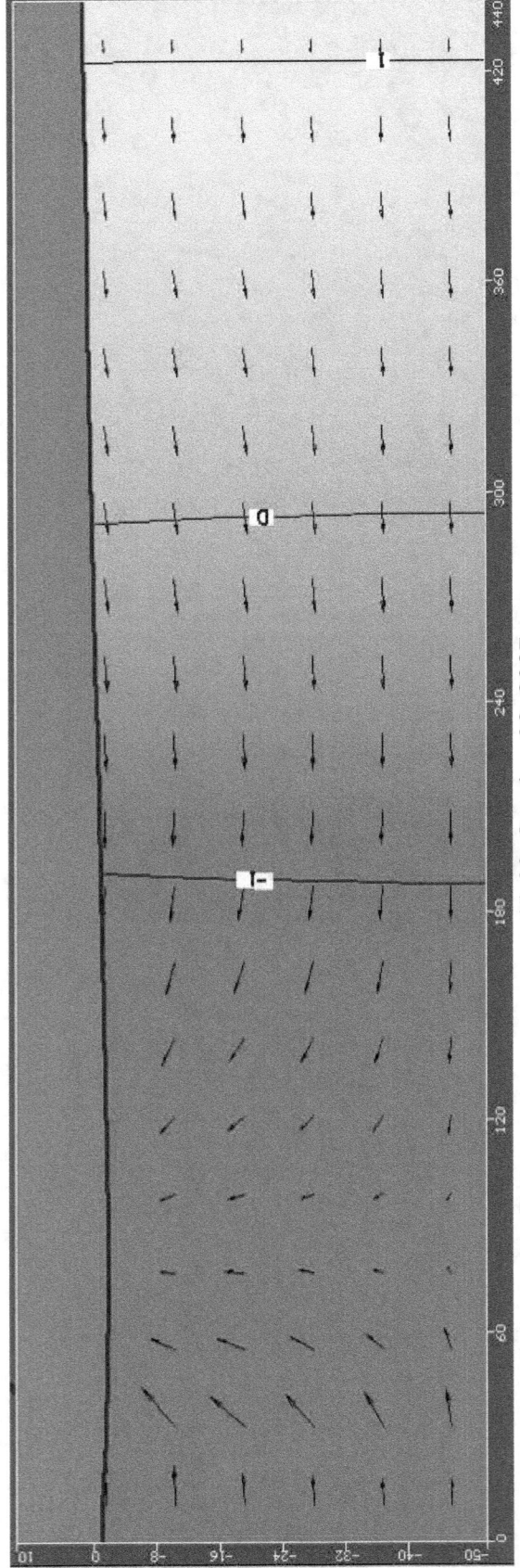

11:30, October 30, 2007

28

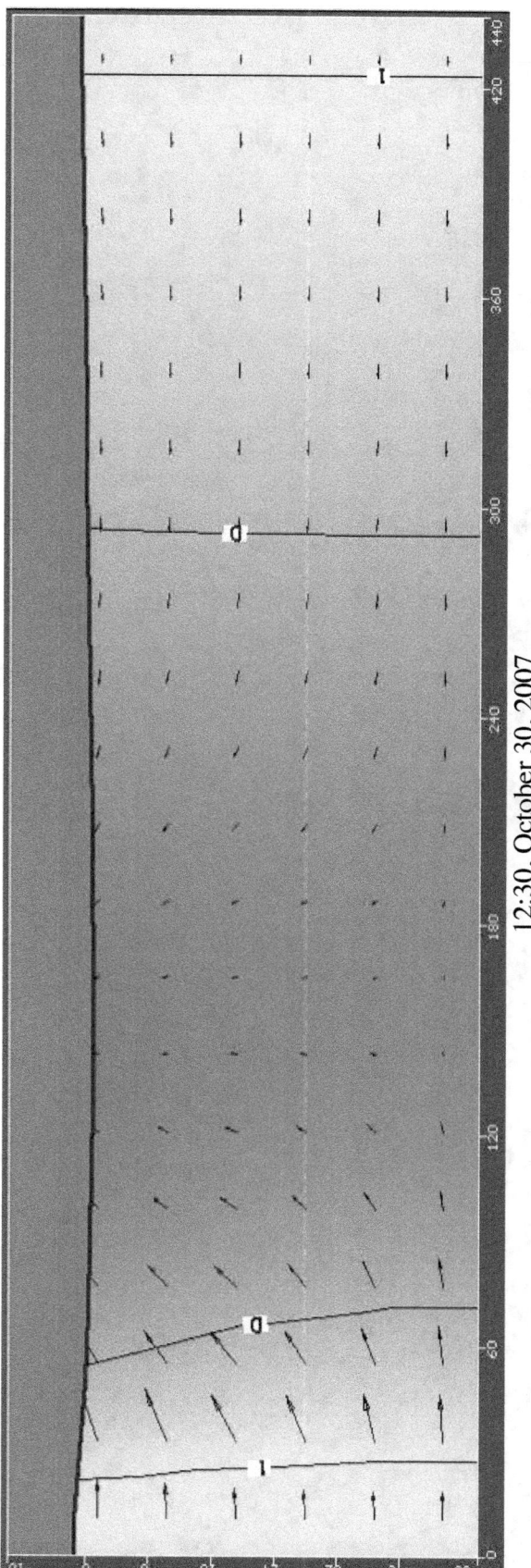

12:30, October 30, 2007

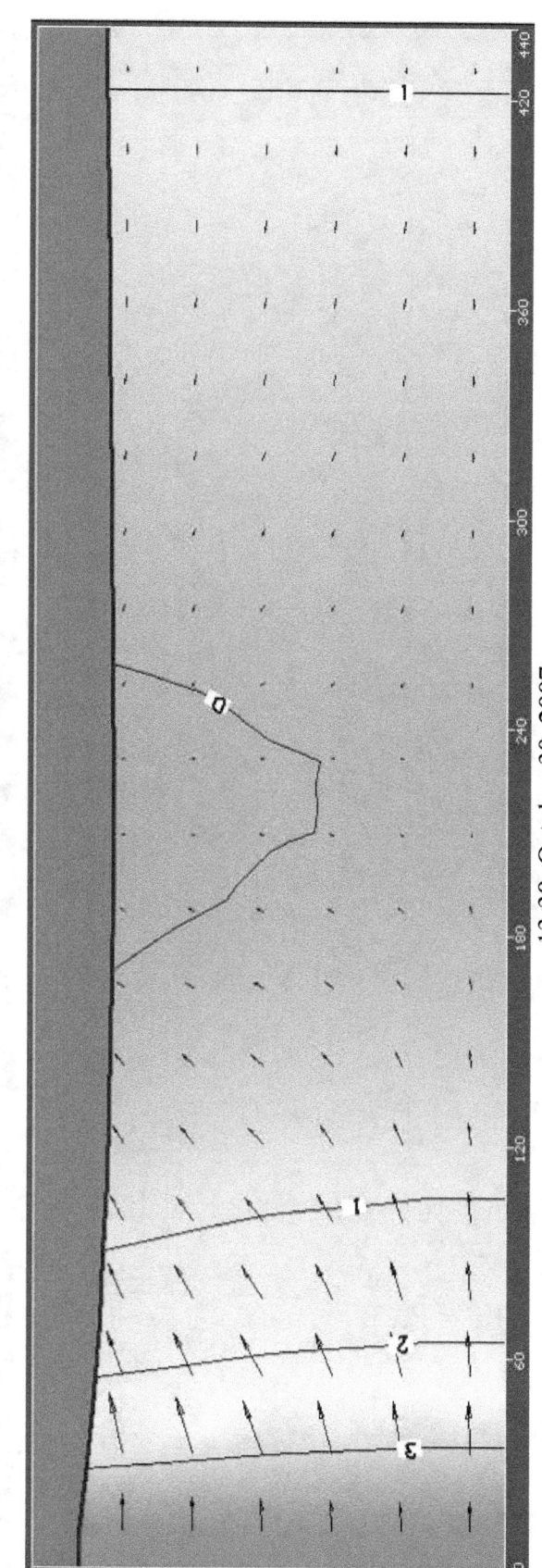

13:30, October 30, 2007

29

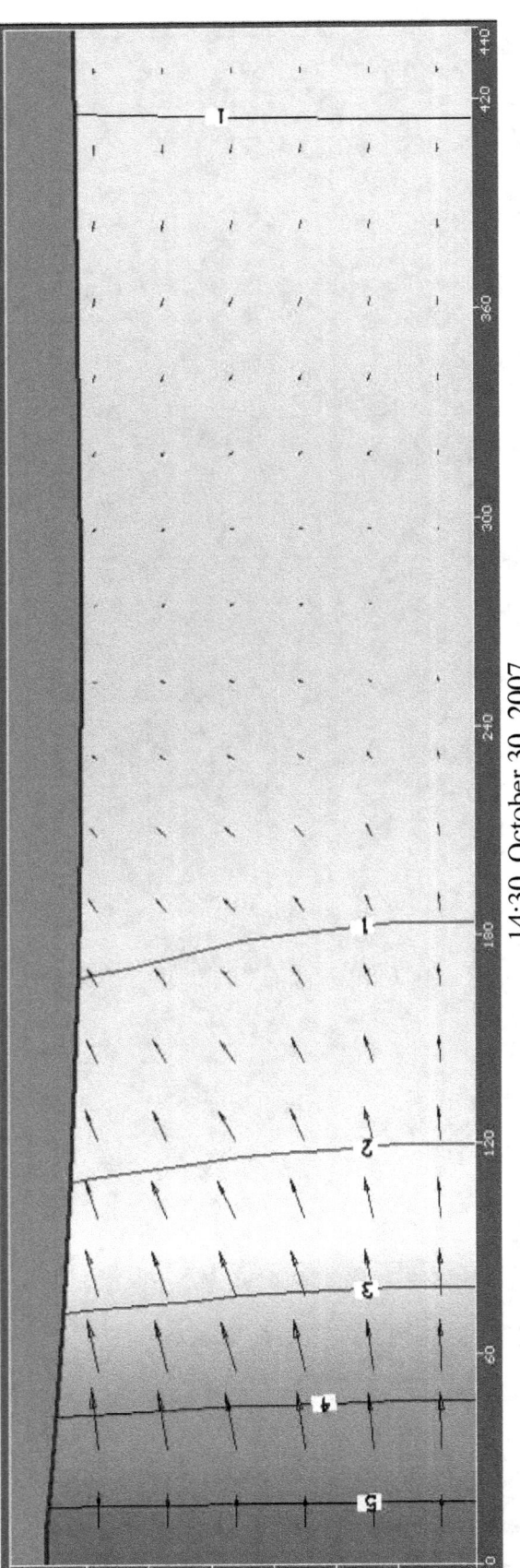

14:30, October 30, 2007

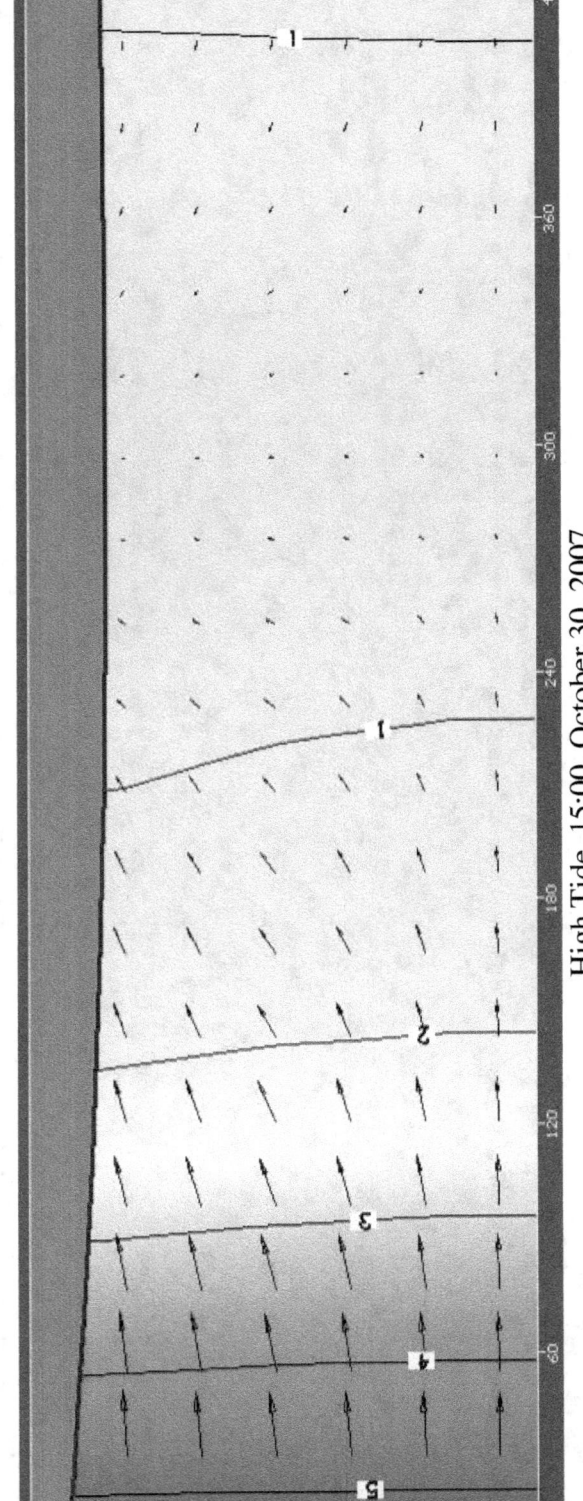

High Tide, 15:00, October 30, 2007

30

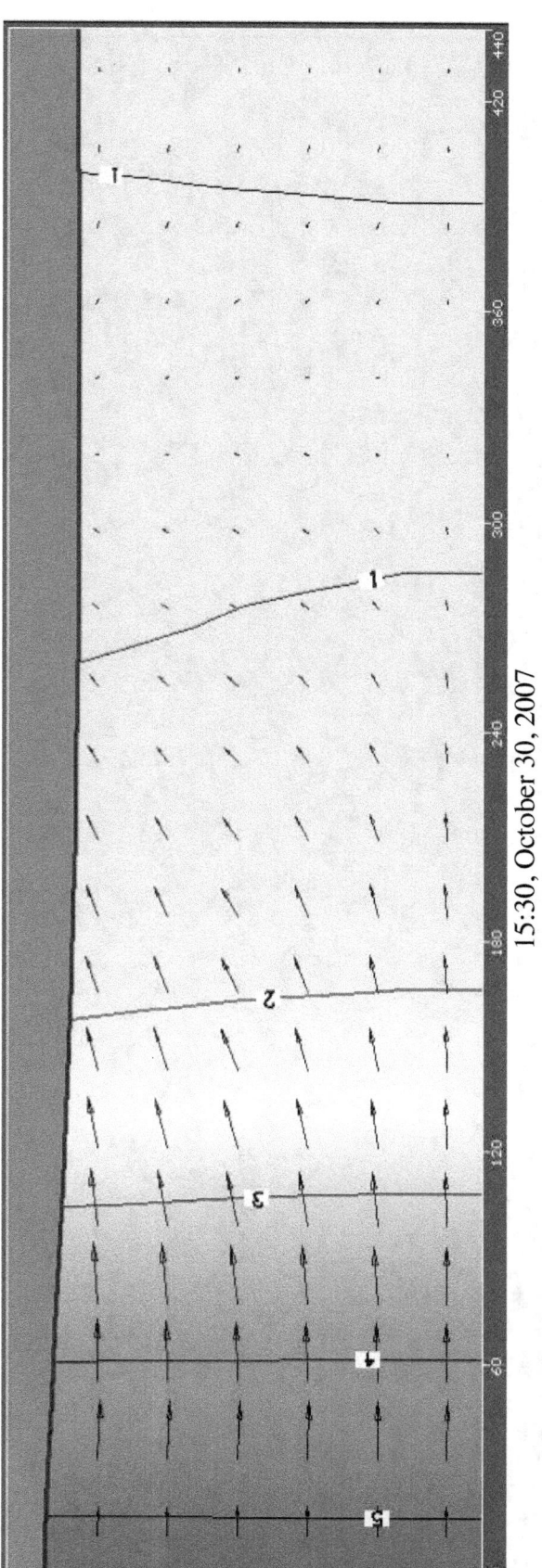

15:30, October 30, 2007

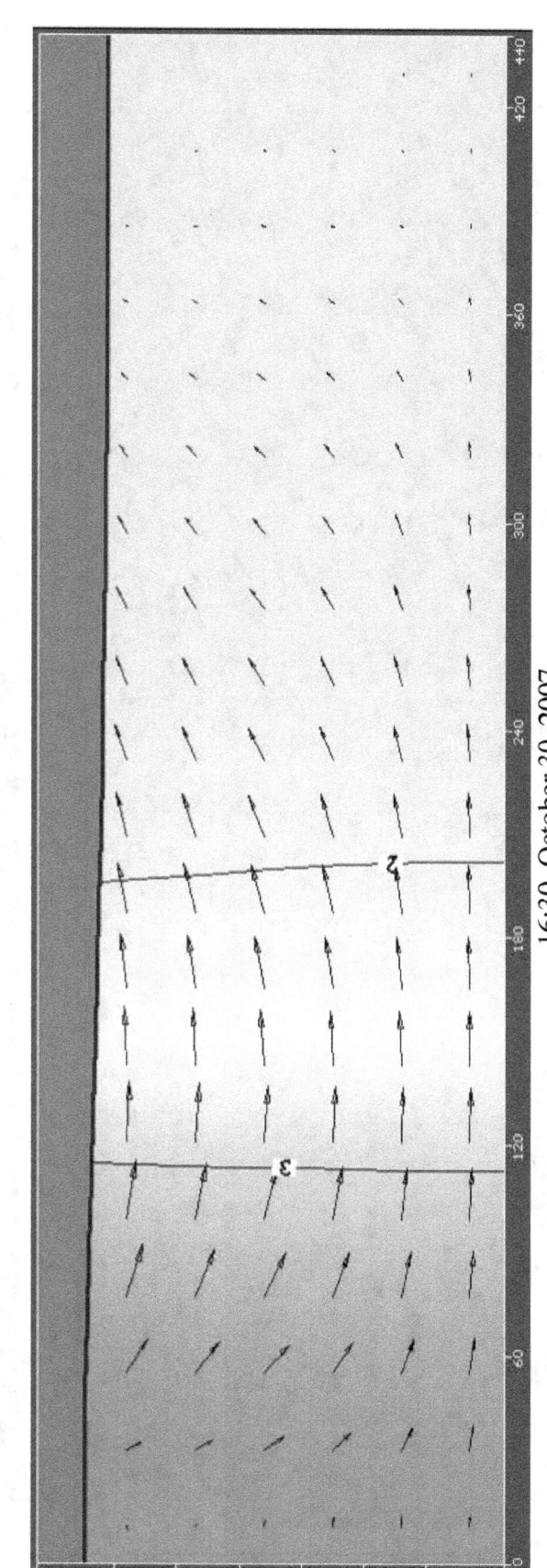

16:30, October 30, 2007

31

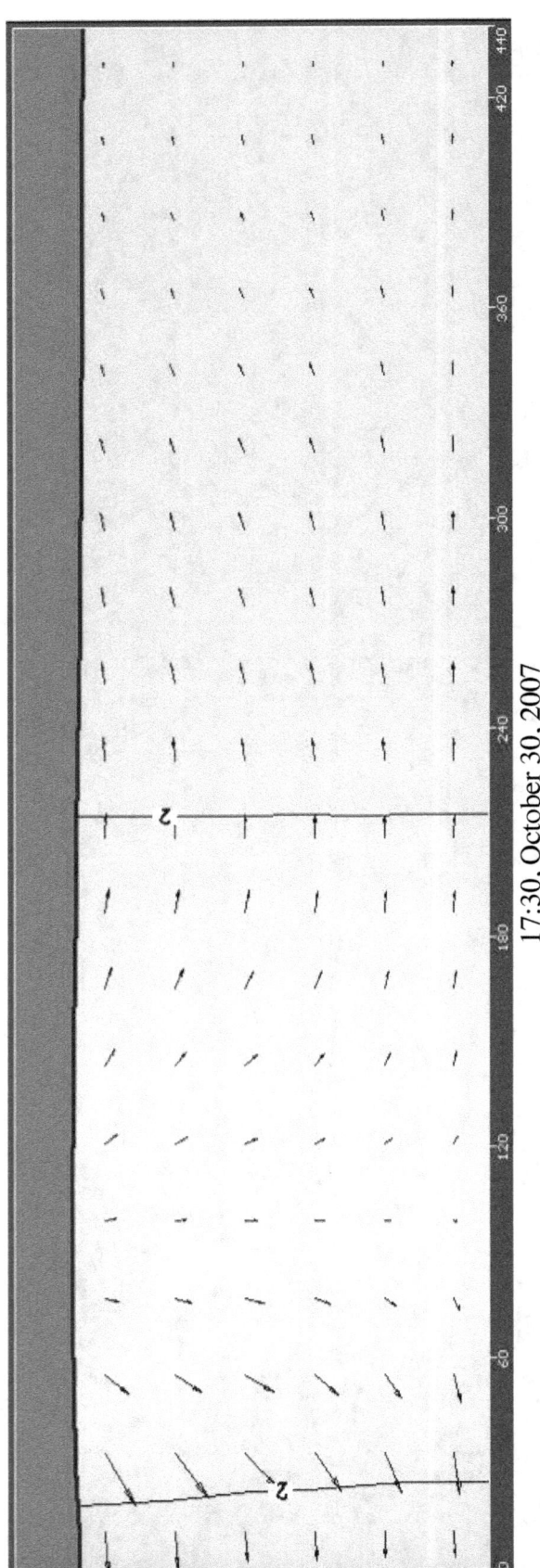

17:30, October 30, 2007

18:30, October 30, 2007

32

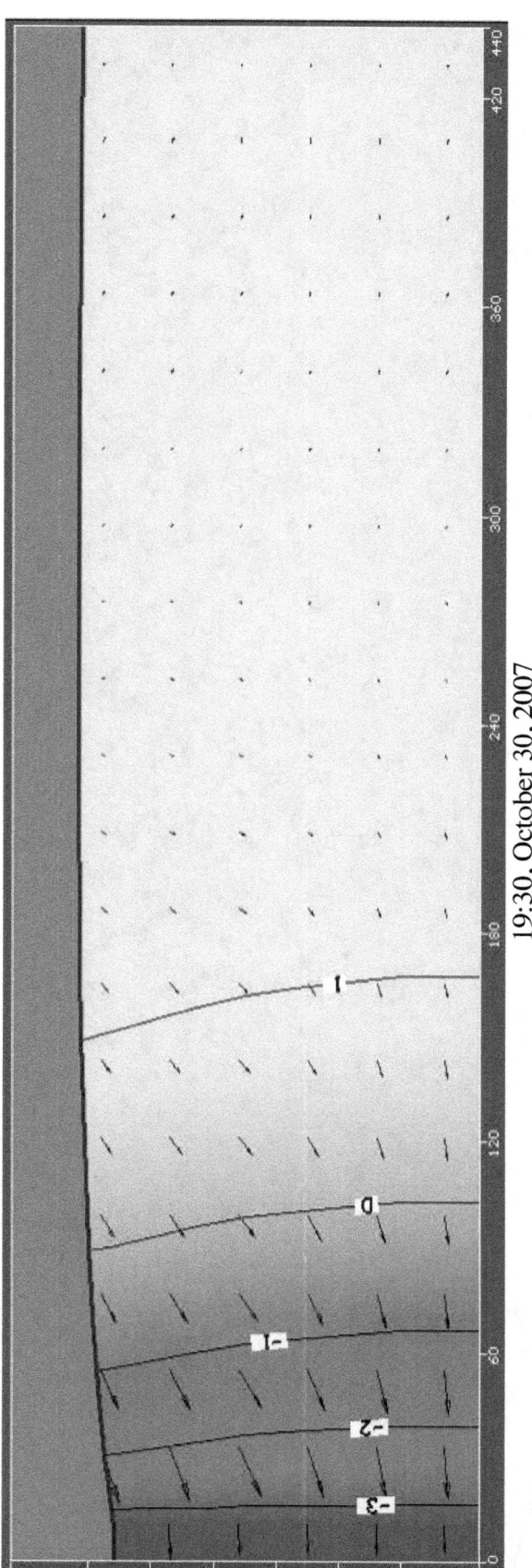

19:30, October 30, 2007

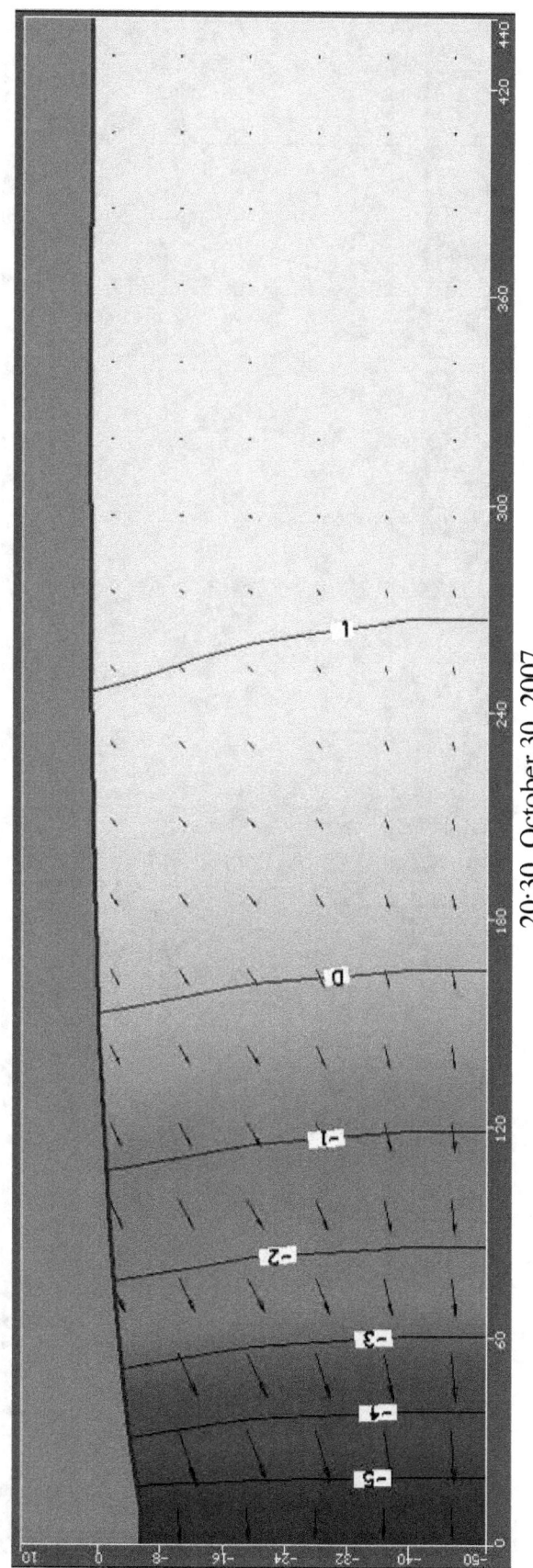

20:30, October 30, 2007

33

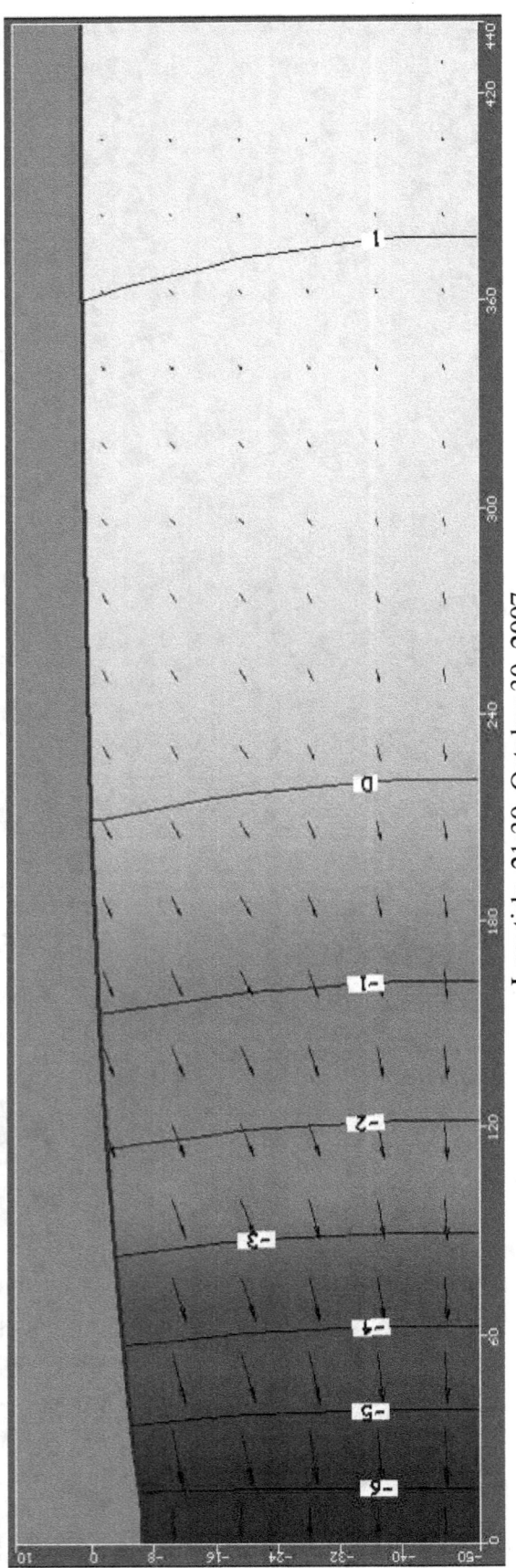

Low tide, 21:30, October 30, 2007

34

NPS D-393, July 2008